THE ART
OF WOOING

Other books by David E. Outerbridge

WITHOUT MAKEUP: LIV ULLMANN
THE LAST SHEPHERDS
THE HANGOVER HANDBOOK

THE ART OF WOOING

A Guide to Love and Romance

• • • • • •

David E. Outerbridge

Clarkson N. Potter, Inc. / Publishers
DISTRIBUTED BY CROWN PUBLISHERS, INC.
NEW YORK

Grateful acknowledgment is made to the following sources for the use of excerpted materials.

Pages 6–7 *The Blue of Capricorn* by Eugene Burdick, Houghton Mifflin Company, 1961.
Pages 12–13 *The Natural History of Love* by Morton Hunt, Alfred A. Knopf Inc., 1959.
Pages 14–15 *Masks of God* by Joseph Campbell, Penguin Books, 1970.
Pages 38–39 *The Unknown Craftsman* by Soetsu Yanagi, Kodansha, 1972.
Page 79 *The Evolution of Human Sexuality* by Donald Symons, Oxford University Press, 1979.
Pages 80–81 *Flaubert in Egypt* by Francis Syeegmuller, Little, Brown and Co., 1973.

Published by Clarkson N. Potter, Inc.,
One Park Avenue, New York, New York 10016 and simultaneously in Canada by General Publishing Company Limited

Library of Congress Cataloging in Publication Data

Outerbridge, David.
  The art of wooing.
  1. Courtship. I. Title.
HQ801.097   1984   306.7′34   83-11168
ISBN 0-517-54935-2

Manufactured in the United States of America
Designed by Ann Gold

10 9 8 7 6 5 4 3 2 1
First Edition

*This book is dedicated to the wife of J.W.S.
(and to J.W.S. himself who
thought it appropriate).*

ACKNOWLEDGMENTS

I would like to thank all the men and women who, by their interest in this book, provided much of its substance. Some are named, others not. A special acknowledgment is due Ivan Kats, who for every book I have written has always had a ready arsenal of literary references. I am also indebted to Morton Hunt for his study, *The Natural History of Love*. From it I have drawn a number of illustrations of the evolution of wooing. I also want to express my gratitude to Carol Southern, the most discerning editor I know.

CONTENTS

Tush, man, thou knowest not how to woo. 'Tis not to be done with time-worn jests and thread-bare sophistries: with quips, conundrums, rhymes and paradoxes. 'Tis an art in itself, and must be studied gravely and conscientiously.

Gilbert & Sullivan,
The Yeomen of the Guard

THE ART
OF WOOING

INTRODUCTION

· · • • • · ·

Every year in Camden, Maine, near where I live, there is a summer-long series of Shakespeare productions performed in the romantic environment of an open-air amphitheater. A few evenings ago, I went to a performance and was struck by the amount of *wooing*. The Bard, in this particular play, deployed the words *woo, wooer,* or *wooing* scores of times. Not only was wooing in the dialogue, it consumed much of the action between assorted couples.

Wooing in these sometimes humorous, sometimes tragic, but always human tales of Shakespeare is a saga of pursuit. However, it is a pursuit not with lances or snares but with attention, testaments of admiration, and devotion.

I think it timely to restore wooing to our active vocabulary and rekindle its attendant actions. There is nothing anachronistic about wooing if for no other reason than we *want* to be wooed as a reassurance that who we are is of interest to others. We all want to be noticed, admired, cared for: we all want to be wooed. We want to be pursued, not as a quarry but with attention, caring, and the romantic impulse. Just as Shakespeare could blow ardor into an encounter between two people, in real life we yearn for similar elevating experiences.

The Art of Wooing is an homage to the word wooing and to the spirit and activity it represents: gestures more powerful than a kiss, emotional connections as complex as a game of chess, an enterprise so heady and satisfying that it may bring into life a rare sense of emotional completeness.

The actual elements of the activity (as will be illustrated) are varied; they range from specific gestures (flowers, letters, declarations) to more basic components (generosity of spirit, a tolerance for uncertainty, sincerity of intention and action—and trust).

As an infant grows into childhood, smiling at the universe, there is a brief period of years when he is generous with his world. Children pick field flowers and happily give them away, offer their toys and smile in the pleasure of doing these little things. This is an age that comes after the self-absorption of babyhood and predates a sense of ownership, an age before the quality of "being careful" has been learned, an age of trust.

Wooing is a magical activity because it brings us back, in an unlikely return, to that childhood age. It is easier to give field flowers, an impromptu gift without consequence, than it is to give trust, of course; but there is a similarity between the two gifts in the generosity of spirit that prompts them. Why is it that, for two wooers, a moment on a beach in the warm fragrance of sand and the light of a full moon brings silence and an increase in the heartbeat? It is because in that sweet silence there is no distance from the childhood buoyancy that comes before ownership and carefulness, and so all that is within the wooers may be expressed with a look or the fleeting touch of one finger against another. Time is called the fourth dimension, but these occasions are outside time, in a fifth dimension of tranquillity.

Many of the satisfactions of wooing have been brushed aside by the current advisers on how to pick up or seduce someone. These pundits only present a drawer full of technical advice. They are scratching at the surface of a subject they never have the time or interest to examine: grating the orange skin and setting aside the orange. What the human spirit yearns for has been turned inside out in the rush to master and secure technique.

Wooing is this: a sublime moment often accomplished with no more than a graceful gesture, the corner of a smile, a moment of attention—little things that cost nothing, each prompted by a feeling of respect and trust.

It is important to distinguish between wooing, flirtation, and seduction. Flirtation is an overt, impertinent (and often insincere) expression of desire or admiration. Seduction or wooing may follow from flirtation, but that one or both will follow is far from predetermined. Seduction is the process by which someone is coaxed to bed and sex. We can seduce someone as part of a process of wooing, but not vice versa, because wooing is a procedure to win someone—the total someone. There are ways of seducing that are more subtle and wily than others, but the intention of gaining sex remains the same. The wooing word or glance that says "I like you" is making a larger statement, even if it is represented by a far more trifling gesture than the seductive move. Innate sexual drive will be part of most wooing, but bed is only part of the pursuit. It is for this reason that wooing is not frivolous. In seduction it is permissible to hyperbolize—to do anything to succeed in conquest. "You have the most beautiful breasts I have ever seen," a seducer says to a girl in a cashmere sweater at a cocktail party. What he really means is, "I want to get my hands on them." A wooer may also say "You have beautiful breasts," but he says this within a mosaic of other considerations. It is a telltale sign that he is smitten and, being human, feels erotic desire. But the desire is for the girl, not the breasts.

In Scotland, the men who trawl for herring say that what they do is "prosecute fish." It is an interesting expression that connotes calculation, cunning, and methodology. Some men can be observed treating women as prey in this manner. Wooing can surely have its strategy, but if women are thought of as herring, to be kippered and canned, the wooing will fail.

It is the unpredictability, singularity, and richness of every person and of the relationship between two people that legitimizes the use of the word *art* in connection with wooing. No computer can predict the course of wooing; wooing is intuitive. The dictionary definition given for art is: "The quality, production, expression, and realm of what is beautiful." The quality, production, expression, and realm of wooing is very beautiful. Without it we are impoverished, only playing in a shallow pond.

When the idea for this book was in its first tentative formation, I tried to describe it to a couple with whom I was having dinner. As I talked the woman became animated. She soon turned to the man she was with, tapped him on the knee and said, "Listen to this, Johnny. This is important!" In the hundreds of conversations I have had with men and women on this subject since then, I have not encountered one dissent from her remark. We need and want to be wooed as much as we want to be bedded.

I do not believe that any book on wooing can be "how-to." Nonetheless there are elements of wooing that can be described and rekindled. Some of them are simple things that may be as concrete as a phone call or as ethereal as "impulse." Other elements are deeper and a measure of the degree to which we have unlocked and opened the doors to trust, respect, and vulnerability. In the search for a full life, with its attendant pleasures (as opposed to "fun"), we need to give time to the power of wooing. It is such a basic need that I believe it overrides any constraint felt to be imposed by women's liberation or by any model of the contemporary self.

D.E.O.
The Hen Islands, July 1983

ONE · · · ·

HISTORY
OF WOOING

· · · · · ·

If wooing is a magical entreaty for another's affection, did it not always exist? Strangely enough, it did not. Wooing is a relatively recent development in male-female behavior. All the descriptive words in current romance fiction have no counterpart in ancient Greece. Nor could such a form of writing have existed there, because wooing did not occur in daily life.

Anthropologists point out that if a word does not exist in the language of a culture, then the emotion or behavior it describes will not exist, either. In some tribal cultures wooing is still not, today, part of the way in which a man and a woman form a relationship, sexual or otherwise.

One day my wife was sitting on a beach outside of Papeete [in French Polynesia, on Tahiti] while I was skin diving. A net fisherman, a big attractive man of about twenty-five, was working the water close to the shore. Perhaps my wife looked lonely. In any case she was alone. The fisherman walked over and said hello to her in French.

"Would you like to make love?" he asked without any introductory remark, and in a very gentle voice "I know a place just behind those trees."

My wife explained that she was only waiting for me to come in from skin diving. He looked out toward the reef and then back at my wife.

"He may be out there for hours," he said simply.

My wife still declined. He was not in the least offended. He pointed out the private place beyond the trees in case we should like to use it. Then he went back to his fishing.

Thus Eugene Burdick describes stark and unembroidered Polynesian mores in the 1950s.

Curiously, in the Norwegian language today there is a word for proposing but none for its antecedent, wooing. Perhaps this points to the directness fostered by the Nordic darkness; it is true that country ways—there and elsewhere—are unambiguous. A ladder was placed against a girl's window. If the shade was up a man might climb and enter; shade down, stay away.

In antiquity, the Greeks had the institution of marriage, but it was no more than a formally arranged contract for housecleaning and procreation. They also had prostitutes, separated into levels of intellectual and social standing. And of course, as is well known, the Greeks were partial to homosexual unions. Today, more than two thousand years later,

Sappho is still the supreme advocate of lesbian sexuality; and Plato and Socrates, although they are studied for their philosophies, can also be read for their nods to the widespread appreciation of pederasty.

In such a context, where sexual needs were amply supplied, it is easy to see why the subtle magic of wooing had gone undiscovered in the making of human ties. Furthermore, the feelings we describe by the word *love* were not part of the Greeks' or, for that matter, the Polynesians', normal emotional experience. The Greeks had two words for love: *eros* and *agape*. *Agape* described spiritual love, and *eros* erotic or carnal love. Men used to fall silent at the sight of a beautiful boy, lust for him, pine for him—and occasionally for one of the *hetaerae* (the aristocratic prostitutes)—but this was not love as we know it today; nor did it produce the concomitant courtship. "Love must not touch the marrow of the soul," Euripedes said—the very opposite of what is expected and believed in twentieth-century America.

In Rome, the next highly evolved Western civilization, customs were somewhat different. If one could say that seduction is equivalent to wooing, then history would show that wooing was born and flourished in Rome. But seduction is only a courtship of the loins. As with the Greeks, homosexuality continued to be a popular outlet for sexual appetite—even for Julius Caesar, about whom it was said (though not normally in first year Latin primers): *Omnium mulierum vir et virorum mulier.* ★ This epithet for the

★"The wife of every man and the husband of everyone's wife."

Romans' greatest leader also points to a major activity of their way of life: adultery. Seduction of someone else's wife was a considerable pastime of the upper classes. "Lesbia," who was the subject of so many of Catullus's rhapsodic poems about sex, was based on a neighboring aristocrat's wife; and the "Corrina" of Ovid's poetry was a catchall figure representing his many illicit conquests.

Ovid wrote books and books of love poems, but he was most appreciated by his reading public for *Ars Amatoria (The Art of Love)*. This book, a combination of pick-up techniques, hygienic advice and sexual how-to, is a blending of Emily Post, Alex Comfort and Alexandra Penney, and a veritable encyclopedia of strategy and tactics. But what is startling is that it is a guide solely to adulterous conquests. Ovid even considered the pros and cons of having sex with a desired married lady's maid (a good person to enlist in the seduction), as a diversion from the principal objective:

Still if she seems a comely lass
And you a trusty helper find her
As through her hands your letters pass,
For second course I do not mind her;
First take the mistress to your arms,
And then enjoy the servant's charms.

Here Ovid discusses the discomforts of a man going to a dinner party at which his mistress and her husband will be present. (The passage is translated into English by Dryden, who, along with his contemporaries, took much pleasure in the advice of ancient Romans in these matters.)

Whene'er you think upon our last embrace,
With your forefinger gently touch your face.
If any word of mine offend my dear,
Pull, with your hand, the velvet of your ear;
If you are pleas'd with what I do or say,
Handle your rings, or with your fingers play . . .
Let not his hand within your bosom stray.
And rudely with your pretty bubbies play.
But, above all, let him no kiss receive!
That's an offence I can never forgive. . . .
These things are plain to sight; but more I doubt
What you conceal beneath your petticoat.
Take not his legs between your tender thighs,
Nor, with your hand, provoke my foe to rise.
How many love-inventions I deplore,
Which I myself have practis'd all before!

. . . and when night is come,
Tuck'd underneath his arm he leads you home.
He locks you in; I follow to the door,
His fortune envy, and my own deplore.
He kisses you, he more than kisses too;
The outrageous cuckold thinks it all his due.
But add not to his joy by your consent,
And let it not be given, but only lent.
Return no kiss, nor move in any sort;
Make it a dull and malignant sport.
Had I my wish, he should no pleasure take,
But slubber o'er your business for my sake;
And whate'er fortune shall this night befall,
Coax me tomorrow, by forswearing all.

Poor Ovid was eventually exiled. He had forgotten one of the very principles of seduction he had advocated: do not get caught, especially if the woman in question is a relative of the emperor. His best-selling handbook on hanky-panky was banned, but Ovid's writings are not banned today, and for those who enjoy reading advice in such matters, these are rich pages.

Following the fall of Rome there came a long period of stagnation in the evolution of male-female relationships. The next, and most important, occurrence was the actual birth of wooing, which took place in twelfth-century France. Furtive, "sinful" sex, combined with marriages built on the conveniences of political alliance and property holdings, were enriched by the budding of courtly love. It was the age when Launcelot and Guinevere were invented, when the tragic love story of Tristran and Iseult was written, when troubadours spread tales of the glories of courtship. It was the century when Héloïse and Abelard, through the true story of their secret marriage made in defiance of the powerful men of their age, opened the doors to passionate love; when it became part of human experience to "fall in love"; when it was discerned that true nobility of soul was necessary in order to undertake and carry through to its end the mesmerizing and terrifying process of love. To love meant to admit vulnerability, to acknowledge emotions and ideals and to expose them, and oneself, to risk of flaying. Courts of Love were established to shape and arbitrate the behavior of wooing.

In all the annals of elaborate and persistent courtship no one has ever surpassed Ulrich von Lichtenstein, a legendary thirteenth-century German troubadour and knight-errant. Undaunted by a lack of positive response from his ladylove, Ulrich spent fifteen long years performing one glorious deed after another in her honor, in order to win her affection.

It is startling to learn that for the first several years of his knightly wooing Ulrich had yet to meet the object of his affection, and when the moment finally arrived she rebuffed him cruelly by refusing to speak with him, ripping out a lock of his hair, and for good measure informing him (through an intermediary) that she found his looks very unattractive. Poor Ulrich had been born with a harelip. This criticism halted him only momentarily, however. He journeyed across Europe to a surgeon to have the lip repaired. Not only was the operation performed without use of anesthesia but he contracted a fever and lay near death for more than a month.

In the years that followed Ulrich wrote songs of love for the lady, in the manner of the troubadours, and sent descriptions of his valorous actions in her name. None of this produced the desired result, and so in 1227 he fashioned a most stupendous display of gallantry. Dressed in the white robes of the goddess Venus he vowed to ride from Venice through the continent dueling with any man who would challenge him.

Morton Hunt, who has chronicled Ulrich's courtship, describes the beginning of the odyssey:

The cavalcade of the putative deity, when it finally hove into view, was worth the wait. First there slowly rode by a dozen squires, extravagantly dressed in white; then came two maids-in-waiting, also gorgeously got up, followed in turn by half a dozen musicians, festively sowing and blowing away; finally there appeared on a luxuriously caparisoned horse a husky man-sized figure, attired in an outrageously ornate white gown, a heavy veil, a pearl headdress, and waist-length pearl-bedecked braids . . . Ulrich von Lichtenstein, knight-errant, jouster of great prowess, *Minnesinger* of some talent, and devoted admirer of an unnamed lady for whose love he was undertaking this superb, arduous, and all but impossible task. The curious poor watched and cheered; noblemen saluted gravely; the ladies, informed by gossip of Venus's real identity, hastened to kiss him warmly at every halt; and impatient knights-at-arms sent their men to him with invitations to combat.

Ulrich arrived in Austria without a defeat to his name, and word of his extraordinary triumph spread through the land. The lady, however, was still not sufficiently impressed.

Was this madness? Perhaps. But in its day it was only an extreme example of the expected rites of courtship. Before Ulrich was finally to win his woman he had yet to demonstrate one more act of obsessive loyalty. In one of his ballads of valorous service he spoke of injury to a finger. Somehow the lady understood that it had been cut off and accused him (again through an intermediary) of deception when she learned that the finger had healed. Ulrich could not bear the thought of such a criticism and forthwith had a friend chop off the finger with a knife. He then had the digit mounted in a golden clasp within a velvet case, and sent it to his love as further demonstration of devotion. Mercifully, the story has a happy resolution. In the end, finally, he was granted the favor that for all those years he sought.

Ulrich may have been obsessed in his service to courtship, but all he did was well within the accepted range of wooing behavior of the day.

It is worth a brief diversion to note that, although the arrangements of courtly love were adulterous, they were always limited to a single partner. In India, of a somewhat comparable period, this was most certainly not the case. The boy-god Krishna had the ability to transform himself into as many boy-gods as he pleased. One evening while he was playing his flute the sound of his haunting melody reached the ears of the sleeping *gopīs* (young wives of cowherds). They left their sleeping places by the thousands and ran to the woods in search of him. Seeing this army of excited women approaching, Krishna conveniently cloned himself into a like number, and the fun began.

As she-elephants, covered with dust, enjoy the frenzy of a great male, so those herding women—their limbs covered with dust and cowdung—crushed about Krishna and danced with him on all sides. Their faces, laughing, and their eyes, large and warm as those of dark antelopes, grew bright as they drank ravenously the wonder of their dear friend. . . . And their hair, coming down, cascaded over their bounding breasts as the young god, thus among the *gopīs,* played, those nights, beneath the autumn moon. . . .

The Lord multiplied his presence and each felt that he embraced her by the neck. The sky above became filled with deities and their wives, gathering to watch; heavenly kettledrums sounded; showers of blossoms began to fall; and the ring of dancers commenced moving to the rhythmic sound of their own bangles, bracelets and ankle bells. With measured steps, graceful movements of the hands, smiles, amorous contractions of the brows, joggling hips, bounding breasts, perspiration streaming and locks of hair coming down, the knots of both hair and garments coming loose, the *gopīs* began to sing. And the Lord Krishna, sporting among them, wonderfully brilliant, cried "Well done! . . ." placing his hands on the various breasts and letting his perspiration rain upon all.

· · •

The era of courtly love came to an end in Europe but in spite of the fact that male-female doings had to endure the ages of Calvin and Victoria, a number of the qualities that blossomed in twelfth-century France never disappeared; and they remain embedded in our psyches today. What the romance fiction of our day is filled with, what the Bills and Jims and Marys and Susans experience in wooing is the heritage of that era:

- lovesickness: the *angst* and mopes of uncertainty
- homage to a woman: no longer is she property or the means to property, but a worthy partner

- passion: the energy that fuels courtship, a yearning simultaneously to win and to surrender, as distinguished from lust that soon is sated in conquest
- the woman in control: the man woos, the woman responds

. . •

Even if romance had its periods of hibernation in succeeding centuries, what was begun in the twelfth century was never completely lost to sight. An interesting example is the following letter (slightly edited from the version quoted by Morton Hunt).

Mine own sweetheart, this is to tell you of the great loneliness that I find here since your departing, for I promise you I think the time longer since your departing this occasion than I was wont to do a whole fortnight. . . . Wishing myself, especially in the evening, in my sweetheart's arms, whose pretty duckies I trust shortly to kiss; written with the hand of him that was, is, and shall be yours by his will.

Who wrote such romantic lines? Casanova? Barbara Cartland? The answer is surprising, and a testament to the legacy of the Courts of Love: Henry VIII to Anne Boleyn (whom he was soon to have beheaded).

Life and literature of the nineteenth and early twentieth centuries were resplendent with a revival of romance and wooing. Romantic heroes and high-spirited heroines abounded in books and plays and finally in the medium of film. The characters of Jane

Austen, Charles Dickens, Henry James, and of the directors William Wyler and George Cukor, wooed for marriage, but they wooed with as much ceremony and seriousness as the chevaliers. Then, as abruptly as the troubadours had introduced the ways of wooing, the culture of the mid-twentieth century trammeled them almost to extinction. The culprits: the Pill, and the coincidence of the Me Generation.

Why should easy and effective birth control do away with all the subtle, beguiling early stages of male-female relationships? "Courtship is nature's method of preventing sexual fatigue," Bertrand Russell once remarked. Courtship might also be seen as nature's way of tempering endless and unwanted pregnancies. Suppose that in the 1950s we had experienced, instead of the Pill, a strange new effect of sunspot activity: a change in human biology that meant that, in spite of all precautions, sexual intercourse was certain to result in pregnancy. Suddenly, women would have been very reluctant to go to bed with men; men would have had to go through long, elaborate demonstrations of affection, care and commitment, usually capped by a proposal of marriage, in order to win their lady. There would have been a prodigious amount of wooing.

The Pill, on the contrary, meant that sex could be enjoyed risk-free, and, as sex is enjoyable, the natural consequence was that many people took full advantage of the new possibilities. A "one-night stand" became the bustling avenue for exploration of the pleasures of sexual activity with large numbers of people. The avenue grew to be very broad indeed, and the change in customs it carved out occurred with extraordinary rapidity. Graduates of college in the late forties and early fifties recall that evening dates and college dances and football weekends might involve what was known as "heavy petting," but full-fledged sex was not a foregone conclusion. Just a few years later, the principal of a coed boarding school could report that within two weeks of fall registration a stroll through the school's adjacent woods on any given afternoon would flush out numbers of mating adolescents. The new permissiveness swept through the country, although for the pre-Pill generation it created a residual nervousness. A pre-Pill man reports that he still finds there is an awkward moment when he is out with a post-Pill woman. His sense of what is okay to suggest the first time out, the second, etc., is quite different from the woman's. "If I say, 'Let's go to bed,' I worry that she'll think I'm only after her body. But if I don't pursue it, she may feel that I don't find her physically attractive."

As the century rolled on, risk-free sex gave rise to a whole universe of sexual variation and sexual explicitness, the reaction to a long repression. The time did not call for wooing, but rather for the promise of sexual brilliance—a promise fed by endless magazines and books, and the legitimation of pornography. We were into the Age of Concupiscence. Neither Masters and Johnson nor the Adam and Eve catalog of sexual paraphernalia is concerned with courtship. As excitement wore off the world became something of a meat market.

Something was gained and something was lost in

all of this. There is only so much time in a day, so much pliancy in a psyche; and if, in male-female relationships, time and heart were given to visions of multiple orgasms, there was little left for romance, wooing, admiration, and love. Women still felt a need for these things; it was served vicariously by romance fiction. *Torrents* of such fiction poured, and still pour, into drugstores and supermarkets, where they are scooped up faster than breakfast cereals. In television ads for these books, sexy men with foreign accents promise the fulfillment of secret dreams; book covers show pictures of wooing couples on storm-wracked coasts, in lush gardens, outside moon-bathed castles.

Romance fiction performs a function parallel to that of an earlier genre of books. In the forties and fifties men and boys used to spend hours reading and rereading contraband pornographic literature. Sometimes it was in book form, sometimes only in typed, dog-eared pages. The most famous of these tracts was, perhaps, *The Green Door,* which passed from hand to hand in school and college corridors. It fulfilled male fantasies and provided a surrogate sexual partner for empty hours. Then real sex became available, and although the books are still read for titillation they are no longer the crucial source they were. In the same way, a return to wooing will bring to real life the fantasies today reposited in fiction.

TWO · · · ·

FEAR
OF WOOING

· · • • • ·

Each season, just as there are scores of romance novels published, there are scores of new books filled with advice about how to make contact with someone new. The success of these books is based on the premise that there is something intimidating about saying hello. Why is this? Need it be that way?

One of the reasons why so many relationships that might be never are is that either the man or the woman is frightened. "What will I say?" "What if she says no?" "What if he doesn't like me?" Often these fears are treated as two separate ailments: the terror of doing it wrong—blurting out the wrong words or being reduced to no words at all—that is, the fear of *inadequacy* and the prideful fear of *rejection*.

. . •

He: I am a maker of war, and not a maker of
    phrases.
    You, who are bred as a scholar, can say it in
    elegant language
    Such as you read in your books of the plead-
    ings and wooings of lovers
    Such as you think best adapted to win the
    heart of a maiden. . . .

She: If you would have it well done—I am only re-
    peating your maxim—
    You must do it yourself, you must not leave
    it to others! . . .

He: I can march up to a fortress and summon the
    place to surrender,
    But march up to a woman with such a pro-
    posal, I dare not.
    I'm not afraid of bullets, nor shot from the
    mouth of a cannon,
    But of a thundering "No!" point blank from
    the mouth of a woman . . .

Henry Wadsworth Longfellow,
The Courtship of Miles Standish

Thus the brave Captain Miles Standish spoke of
both fears; both fears are actually of the same cloth.
For the fear of inadequacy—I'm not pretty or witty
enough—is only a preambulary fear of rejection. It is
a fear worth consideration, as is any fear, to see if it is
well grounded, or whether it can be eliminated.

We talk about conquering our fears, and we do
conquer them. Often they are irrational and are treated by the introduction of a shock: if you throw
someone who is terrified of water into it, sometimes

the fear will disappear forever. When the hero of *The Bridges at Toko-Ri* was shaking with fear of the following day's mission, he went and stood in front of the hydraulic launching ram. It would hurtle toward him and stop just inches from his face. That procedure might not calm everyone, but confronting danger did calm him. When CBS moved its employees into a beautiful new skyscraper on Fifty-second Street in Manhattan, staff members on the upper stories were bothered by the fact that the windows went to the floor. Standing next to one of them, looking down on the sidewalk and street eighteen stories away, was fearsome. The firm that had designed the building sent over an architect. He gathered the staff together, explained that no one could "fall out" and then, to the horror of everyone present, raced across the room and hurled himself against the plate glass at full speed. "You see?" he said, straightening himself up after the impact. There was gaping silence. But since that day, some of the fear is gone.

In these examples, however, we are speaking of fears of physical damage or death. In wooing, the fear is of damage to self-image, and this fear is conquered in a different way. A person who has studied a foreign language is often very reluctant to speak it to a person for whom it is a native tongue. The student is fearful that his pronunciation or grammar may be wrong: that he'll make a fool of himself. However, as he quickly learns after he *does* begin to speak, a speaker of a foreign language is flattered by the attempt to communicate with him on his own terms and will encourage the student. Presto, the fear is gone; practice makes for boldness, and so it is with wooing.

Inadequacy is a self-perception and once recognized as such is baggage that can be unpacked and discarded: it will no longer be necessary to hide within silence or a charade.

In the late 1940s there was a young man at Harvard College named Rinehart. He was a solitary type and felt that he had no friends. And although he had lived some eighteen years with an adequate enough sense of self to gain admittance to the college, once there he became obsessed with the fear that the freshman community would ridicule him because he had not immediately become a part of some carousing fraternity or club. So at night he used to go out of his dormitory and, standing in the courtyard, call upward toward his window: "Rinehart? Hey, Rinehart, what are you up to? Want to do something?" He did this a few times a night. After a while people started looking out of windows to find out who all these people were who were always calling up to old Rinehart. But because it was night and he often changed his voice, his ruse succeeded. People began to drift down to the Yard (as the center campus is called) to see whether someone was organizing a party.

The following year, in the way of the Harvard system, Rinehart moved to a new dormitory down by the Charles River. However, in the freshman quadrangle the call "Rinehart" endured. It was a way to bring a group of people to the windows and outdoors. Pretty soon the cry "Rinehart" could produce not just a group but a *crowd*. By the early fifties the call "Rinehart" could trigger the arrival of thousands in the Yard and the potential of a *riot*. It became so serious that the campus police decreed that anyone caught yelling "Rinehart" in the Yard was subject to suspension from the college.

There is a moral to that story. Because he was afraid of ridicule and rejection, in fact, of being alone, he spent a year calling to the wrong person. Instead of calling to Sarah or Laura whom he sat next to in class, or to John or Steven down the hall, he spent a year calling to himself, and he remained alone.

Why are people shy or bashful? The answer is this: they have placed such importance upon the value of what they propose to do that they become crippled by the fear that it may not come out perfectly, as intended. But most often no one else attaches such importance to these things. A person who becomes fearful of the appearance he will make at dinner or a dance and spends hours planning and then changing his clothes is weighing the details of his dress with an importance that none of the other diners or dancers would think of ascribing to it. An orchestra conductor may be nervous, not fearful, of the performance he is about to give. So, too, may an opera star, with the television lights warming up around her. But these people are about to embark on a ninety-minute demonstration of great complexity and drama, before an audience of thousands, even millions. What does that have in common with fearing to say, if a woman looks pretty, "You're very beautiful!"

Enough of these books with their chapters on great opening lines. To have an arsenal of lines in the memory bank already places far too much importance on the objective fact of an encounter. They create more of the very problems they are trying to solve.

A very short story. Every morning Billy Bashful takes a bus to work, on which also rides a girl he thinks he would like to meet. So he studies the chapter "How to Make Contact" and learns thirty lines that seem as if they might be useful. But then, on the bus, while pretending to read the morning paper, he becomes so tied up with the choice of which line and what intonation to use and when to use them that the words are never stuttered out. Or, in what could almost be a scene from a romantic farce, he finally screws up courage enough to say:

"Hi. Pretty weather for a change." He has forgotten in his nervousness to look out the window, but it so happens that it is raining.

She, thinking he is being witty: "Yes, picnic weather, all right."

He, stuttering: "Do you like roast lamb?" (A line actually suggested in one of these manuals.

She, startled by the question: "Yes. But who can afford it?"

He, because opening-lines chapters cruelly never include development of themes, must now either resort to yet *another* line from the book: e.g., "I love soccer games," or else plunge into extemporaneous repartee. In either case, although the latter *would* work if only he were not entwined in an overall fear of this dangerous undertaking, Billy has probably blown it.

Suppose, however, that Billy is touched by the Fairy of Wooing at her question. He would be relieved of all his trepidation and, being normally gregarious, would respond (according to what type of fellow he is) in one of the following ways:

(pragmatically) "But do you realize that hot dogs, by the pound, cost almost as much—more, if you factor in the thirty percent nonmeat products they contain?"

(flirtatiously) "By the way you dress and look I would say you can buy it any day."

(cynically) "Everyone is on food stamps."

(earnestly) "Not me, and I can't think what made me ask you that. I hate lamb. When I was little I had to help my father kill sheep."

(revealingly) "I can on occasion. I especially love it the way the French cook it with flageolets."

(wittily) "Only the shepherds."

(snobbishly) "Certainly not the bus driver."

· · •

The fear of inadequacy or rejection, which is to say the fear of failure, is created by an erroneous attribution of importance to outward aspects of the moment. This sense of importance is generated by ego. We do not want to be slighted, hurt, or seen to be somehow less than ideal. We guard ourselves against these possibilities, and, in the process, against growth. In other words, we are scared to allow ourselves to be vulnerable in a situation. Certainly there are occasions in work or love or play when it is important that we protect ourselves from being wounded. But at least in the early stages of wooing there is no such need. If we present ourselves as we are, refuse to play a role, we cannot be seen and judged summarily. "Can I give you a ride home from the party?" "No." There is no damage done there—possibly only a twinge of regret. And the answer might have been yes.

Fiona meets a man at a dinner party. She hopes that he will call her in the following days. But he doesn't. A friend suggests that perhaps he is shy; why doesn't she call him? Fiona musters up her courage and invites him to the movies. He accepts. But a little while later he calls back to say that he accepted on impulse but cannot go; he has a girl friend of long standing. Fiona tells her friend she is "devastated," but she's not. Her ego is not even bruised. She was not in love, has not lost someone she loved, and she is overlooking the fact that the man felt pleased and he accepted. She makes herself believe that his call has somehow been a rejection of her. In fact, nothing was lost, and perhaps something was even gained.

Fear of failure has been injected into the national consciousness in matters of male-female encounters. Although it's less visible than herpes, it has become an epidemic. "Good in bed" is the genesis of the Big Scare. "Do I perform well?" has become such a crippling question that men become impotent and women feel they have to fake orgasm to evade the question. In matters of wooing, the fear of failure also reaps a terrible harvest. If someone is madly in love and after a long and ardent courtship asks "Will you marry me?" and the answer is no, there is cause for powerful grief. But then it is *grief,* not fear of failure. Moreover, that situation will come, if it comes at all, very late in the cycle of wooing. We are still with the initial encounter: how to say hello.

We are a nation of salespeople and convention-goers. A person goes to an annual convention with his or her product line; there are meetings, displays, symposia, get-togethers of the folks in the industry. Hundreds of people are met for the first time at these occasions. Jack meets Bill, meets Susan; Mary meets Louise, meets Fred. Introductions and conversations come easily. The reason is simple: the common ground is shoptalk.

In *all* encounters between man and woman it is important to remember that a common ground is always present in two forms. First, it never takes long to find a common experience or interest about which two people can prattle for hours. (A sociologist once made a study that showed that any two people in the United States are connected through not more than five other people. Thus a man and a woman meeting for the first time each knows someone who knows someone who knows the one the other knows. If he and she meet at a cocktail party, the number is reduced to one: their host.) Isn't it true that frequently in conversation with a stranger a mutual friend is discovered during the talk?

The second common ground is the encounter itself. Why is it that on airplanes complete strangers so often wind up in long, ardent conversations during the flight? It is because there is the common moment of the flight, a common destination and also proximity of seating. On the plane trip no one is worrying about what to say, or whether he or she is attractive enough to risk speaking.

Anytime two people's eyes first meet, the people should respond as they would on a plane trip. Proximity is easy, common ground is at hand, and if you feel those first warm tingles of attraction it is time to woo.

THREE · · · ·

WHO WOOS WHO

· · · • · · ·

You'll learn tomorrow how we retreated to dhraw thim on before we made them trouble, an' that's what a woman does.

> Rudyard Kipling,
> "The Courting of Dinah Shadd"

"I can't call him; he's going to have to call me."

"Does he have your number?"

"I suppose so."

"But what if he doesn't? He won't be able to reach you. And perhaps he's trying to."

"Well, that would be too bad. I can't be the first to call."

"Well, send a postcard."

"Even worse. Are you out of your mind?"

A conversation in 1984. It is consistent with the history of wooing. From the first flowering of courtship in the twelfth century, it has been the woman who awaits the satisfactory man, accepts or rejects him; in a word, it is the man who is the suitor. The woman controls the progress of the courtship once it has begun, encouraging or tempering the male advance. Historically, she does not initiate, she responds.

The structure of wooing has its own delicate symmetry. Beneath the admonishments "You are very fresh," "Certainly not," etc., a man may discover that a woman is assenting to and encouraging his wooing. In the heyday of courtly love in France, a man knew he was *expected* to persevere in his pursuit of the lady's favors, no matter what obstacles she placed in his way, no matter how indifferent she appeared to be to his attentions.

Today the ritual and code of wooing are much more direct: instead of going off to distant lands to fight a battle in a woman's honor a man requests a date. Still, the same fundamental principles apply, and they still are not principles upon which one can dictate any preset formula of action. "However she does it, a woman has to let a man know that his wooing is effective. She shows this with a blush, with the eyes, with a touch that says 'Tell me more. I like this.' " That is the comment of one woman who wants the wooing but cannot quite bring herself to initiate escalations of the program.

How has women's liberation changed this in recent decades? It is very interesting; one would imagine, or at least I did as I started interviewing for this book, that one of the liberties women would now cherish would be the ability to abandon the role of respondent and to enjoy the freedom of making initiating moves—not to be obliged to wait for a man to woo and then apply a meter to the dance. Almost without exception, however, this was *not* the case among the women with whom I spoke. In fact, even women who were otherwise assertive in the liberation of their sex wanted to be wooed. They talked of yearning for chivalry in a man. The traditional goals and hopes endured. The examples they cited were not from the etiquette books, the superficial traditions of *politesse*. A man who walks on the curb side of a woman as they proceed down a street is bestowing a courtesy that has lost its purpose.

"A man who shows in little ways that he is concerned for my comfort and protection is making me feel very feminine, and I love it. I want him to adore me for who I am, but I also want the gesture that says 'I am doing this because you are *a woman*.' It isn't condescending. It's lovely." This is a modern woman talking.

In a way, both statements bring the issue of women's liberation full circle. Feminism began to redress many inequalities. But it also introduced a new concept: "man" and "woman" were neutered into "person." However, women most often do not want to be wooed as "persons"—they want to be wooed as women. The words often used to characterize the qualities of wooing are *gentleness, attention,* and even that awful word *pampering,* and women find nothing condescending in these things, unless they are carried too far—beyond affectionate gestures into domination and contempt, which of course are antithetical to wooing's spirit of respect. In fact, many women speak of the long hollow period when feminist polemics, which were partly sexual, stripped away gallant, generous behavior, and, as a result, life and love were less.

Nora Ephron writes in her novel *Heartburn:* "Their [divorced] wives went out into the world, free at last, single again, and discovered the horrible truth: . . . that the major concrete achievement of the women's movement in the 1970s was the Dutch Treat."

A man and a woman come out of an apartment building and hail a cab. It stops. The man opens the door and gets in first. The woman climbs in and closes the door. She reaches over and gives the man a kiss on the cheek. "That was wooing," the woman says. There is nothing sillier than for a man to hold open the door of a car and have a woman, especially if she is in a tight skirt, squirm her way across the seat so that he can follow her in. "He was thinking on my behalf, and I'll tell you, it made me feel *wonderful.*"

One should step away from old-fashioned formalities built on obsolescent reasoning. Swill from windows is not relevant to how a couple walks; the tradition that a man gets into a taxi last is a holdover from the days when men helped ladies climb up into carriages.

Perhaps even in elevators the order should change.

In the navy a launch is boarded by enlisted men first, then by officers in order of increasing rank. The captain boards last and always alights first. It is part of RHIP (rank hath its privileges). Who wants to be first into an elevator, to be pressed against the wall by other passengers? Better to get in last and be right at the door to exit when the door reopens. Let conventions, restrictions, and rituals that were appropriate to another age be replaced by instinct, or as thoughtfulness dictates.

Does this kind of abandonment of traditional custom also mean that women will become wooers? The answer is that they probably will not do so more than they have done. However, it can be argued that women *do* woo.

"Who says that men are the wooers?" one woman asks. "You are wrong if you believe it is the man who makes the moves and gives the signals while the woman only responds with approval or disapproval. Women woo men just as much as men woo women. The difference is that when women woo men, the men usually don't notice. They are not just missing signals; very often they are missing the central emotions of the wooing itself. Why? Maybe because they are so concerned with the stereotype, the macho thing, that they can't accept that a woman is advancing the wooing, in her own way, to him. I don't mean to say that what I do is subtle, necessarily, and that the man is missing the subtlety, because that might sound as though I were making a feminist comment. I'm not. I'm saying that women are very much attuned to and observant of the wooing of a man; men, in their turn, are very often not, and they miss the opportunity to experience that click of recognition. Cinderella wooed—when she left behind her slipper, I believe it was the wooing fairy that made her do it. She knew that the man would pursue her; she wanted him to. That is a woman's way of wooing."

There is, however, another perspective—within it, women do all the wooing. Just as the flower woos the insect and the insect does not woo the flower, so there is an efficient logic in courtship. If the flower stopped sending its messages, the insect would have lost one of its important reasons for existence, its patterns of flight, its source of sustenance. When the Me Generation ushered in a decade of self-centeredness, men stopped wooing and being wooed. At first there was no portent of disaster; but soon it became obvious that men and women were missing something special and essential to well-being. The women were the more explicit losers in the demise of wooing, but men and women both will be direct beneficiaries of a return to wooing. And in a certain sense, it is women who will revive it—by sending signals to show that they're receptive to it.

A man is sitting at a table in a café. A woman is walking up the street. He watches her approach, enjoys the way she walks. He smiles at her. She notices this and she smiles back. Then she is past and gone. It was throwaway wooing, as there was no context for its continuation. But his smile was a gesture of pleasure, and her smile was of recognition, encouragement, and a return of his pleasure in her.

As the phrase goes, it takes two to tango; and when we stopped wooing a world fell apart. Men were separated from women, and even sex could not bring them fully together.

"If a man seriously woos a woman, shows in all he says that he cares for her, that she is the center of his thoughts, no woman is going to deny him." This was spoken by a man, and three women and another man who heard the statement thought it was very egotistical. But a fourth woman, reflecting on it for a while, said, "What he says is true. It is what we want."

Wooing comes after desire. Desire is pleasurable. She who causes desire finds her power pleasing. A circle is established. Desire leads to wooing, which leads to pleasure, which heightens the desire and leads to more ardent wooing.

Who, then, woos whom? Men woo women and women give something back that is not less; and from this exchange there radiates the desire for more wooing.

FOUR · · · ·

THE ELEMENTS OF WOOING

· · • • • ·

The art of wooing, like all art, cannot be done by formula. It occurs when the creative spirit gives it life and shape. Prescriptions, by their definition, contain set amounts of ingredients that cannot be altered. Prescriptions won't work for wooing: without the freedom to react to unknown situations, both wooer and "wooee" will be disappointed, stalled—like Billy Bashful.

It is the failing of advisory columns and books on sex that they deny this creativity and freedom, leading the poor aspirant into a doomed world of formulas. Formulas are appropriate in mechanical procedures—in knitting (purl one, knit two) or in tightening down compression heads (set torque at 45 foot-pounds). Sometimes sending flowers will be a pleasant, effective part of courtship, but flowers can also be *pro forma*. Susan: "If a man sent flowers because he wanted to think of me going home to an apartment smelling of jasmine or roses, I would be very touched. I would love him for that. But if he sends flowers because it's Valentine's Day, I'm less sure whether he is thinking of me or of Valentine's Day, and it doesn't woo me in the same way."

An elementary-school teacher I know, when asked, "What textbooks will you be using this year?" responded, "How do I know? I have not met the children yet." In wooing, it is likely there will be patterns, and many of the elements described below will probably be a part of them. However, wooing is particular in every case; and wooing will be its own teacher. No two people will woo each other quite as will another pair, and if each person subsequently woos someone else that experience will be different too. Sometimes the spark of wooing will be the hope of sexual union; sometimes of a lasting emotional relationship; sometimes of the warmth of comradeship; sometimes simply the hope of the thrill of a brief and vivid encounter. What develops may be different from the initial expectation. For this reason wooing cannot be preplanned; and also because set patterns are lifeless, they fail.

(That is not to say there cannot be calculated wooing. See Element 15. But even calculated wooing must move within the overall flow of emotions natural to courtship.)

· · •

In Japan there once lived a Zen monk named Ma-tsu. One day as he sat in meditation, his teacher, Nan-yueh, happened along and asked what he was doing. Ma-tsu replied that he was practicing Zen contemplation. His teacher asked him the reason, and Ma-tsu responded: "Because I wish to become a Buddha." Nan-yueh thereupon bent down and picked up a shard of tile that was lying on the ground. He began to polish it. A brief dialogue followed:

Ma-tsu: "Master, what are you going to make?"

Nan-yueh: "A mirror."

Ma-tsu: "But you cannot make a mirror out of a tile by polishing it, can you?"

Nan-yueh: "Nor can you become a Buddha by Zen contemplation."

ELEMENT 1 ᐧ ᐧ ᐧ

Giving

Any discussion of the elements of wooing must open with giving.

Male empidid flies employ gaudy gifts to woo their mates. Sometimes they offer prey, which they encase in glistening balloons they have manufactured for the purpose. These ostentatious gifts are usually larger than their own little bodies. Tugging one of them up to a female presents a very conspicuous homage; and while the female's attention is captured by the procession and the gift, the male is able to mount her and copulate. Others of the species fill their balloons with brightly colored objects—cheerful petals or scraps of paper—wee baubles.

In human wooing, it isn't necessary to fashion eye-catching gifts or purchase them at great expense, although there will be times when the spirit moves us to do so. Giving can be little things, intangible things.

It can be only a charged look.

It *can* be a flower, but a letter is better.

It can be courtesy, as Alfred Lord Tennyson said, "For courtesy wins woman all as well/As valor may."

It can be flattery. "Employ soft flatteries, and words which delight the ear," counsels the pontiff, Ovid. But is it necessarily true that "A man shall win us best with flattery"? Flattery carries a note of exaggeration with it, and thus also the danger of being perceived as not truly spoken, as just a flirtation.

Giving has to do with time. Maybe not time of Ulrich von Lichtenstein's dimension, the better part of life; but if the wooer's feeling is that "part of me is for you," then this gift will be bestowed even when it doesn't coincide with convenience.

There should be attention. The person who suggests walking leisurely through the park to the movies but who has failed to notice that the woman he's with is wearing high heels is paying court but is not paying attention.

Giving can be a lifetime.

Giving can be an extravagant gesture, which need

not be costly: meeting a woman you wish to woo at the airport rather than when she arrives downtown.

Giving is an activity of many elements in combination, just as wooing is.

ELEMENT 2 · ·

Impulse

It is important to act in accordance with our natures—not to preprogram. This advice is supported by the fact that some of the most affecting and memorable moments in wooing are in the unexpected gestures that occur. They are things done extemporaneously, and the impulse makes them beautiful.

Among the great crested grebe (an aquatic, ducklike bird): he is swimming on the pond, searching for edibles. Some distance away, she is doing the same thing. After a time she calls out a few notes; he keeps on with his pursuit, and she repeats her song. This time he straightens up and looks toward her, dives into the water and disappears.

She changes her posture; she rearranges her wings, her ruff becomes erect, her breast puffs out, and her entire appearance becomes wonderfully striking. He swims under her and emerges a few feet on the far side of her. He shoots straight up from the water. At the beginning of this maneuver he is facing away from her. But gradually he turns in the air, until at the top of his ascension, when his feet are barely still in contact with the water, he has completed his turn and is facing her.

It is a beautiful courtship. Her preparations are less interesting than his. What he has done has been both subtle and unexpected: subtle because he did not pop from the water next to her and clumsily mount her back; unexpected because of his slow turn to look at her in the middle of his dramatic arrival by her side.

In the course of writing this book I was told three stories of wooing—successful wooing—that are each a tale of impulse and the unexpected.

The first: He and she have met occasionally, and although there is attraction and the prospect that a romance might begin, as yet it hasn't. Each is aware of the other; there have been moments of flirtation at cocktail parties when they meet, but their expression of interest in each other somehow has never become distinct. Then on February 6, last, he sends her roses, for no reason other than that he wants to send them, in the clear and time-honored way of saying "I'm thinking of you." The flowers arrive and she calls him, filled with the pleasure of surprise, and they have dinner together that night. She feels she has begun to be wooed. And the reason, she said later, was the warm flush of surprise, of excitement, of regard for his thoughtfulness that she felt when she opened the box and read his brief note. If he had sent them a week later, on Valentine's Day, the roses would not have had the same effect. It does not matter whether their dinner led to lasting love or even a short and happy union; the flowers opened all the possibilities, and they gave themselves a chance.

Second story: A man loves a woman and she knows it. She feels a little bit in love with him, but the outcome is not certain. She is having a small party—cocktails and snacks for friends—and he is invited. He arrives bearing a huge wheel of Cheshire cheese. The generosity and simplicity of the impulse moves her very much. However, amid the bustle and banter of the guests, she only gives him a hug and says thank you. But his was an act of wooing with a consequence. For the rest of the evening, even as she talks with others and especially as she watches them munching on the cheese, she thinks of him and becomes more and more desirous of the moment when they can be alone together. When finally they are, her first words are, "You know, I love you"—a surprise to her, perhaps, as much as it is to him. Cheese has not brought her feelings for him to the surface, the unexpected has. And they are now living happily forever after.

Third story: He and she are in each other's thoughts all the time; in each other's arms part of it. One day he does a corny thing. On the front page of the *New York Times,* where little two-line messages about home delivery and television rentals routinely appear, he places the following reader's notice:

SUZANNE. I ADORE YOU: WILL YOU MARRY ME? DOUG

Some might argue that the ad forsakes the spirit of the romantic proposal of old: the ardent entreaty, the bended knee. The effect, however, is the same. The proposal, made secretly before two million readers of the *New York Times,* is the expression of a true hope, transmitted in a fervid and very unexpected way, and it advanced a romance into marriage.

Flowers, a cheese and an advertisement. In the grand scheme of romance, what do these things have in common? Very little; only the first of them would be part of any list in the standard columns of romantic advice. But each was an expression of impulse, and each, by its unexpected delivery, was an act of wooing that was appreciated and reciprocated.

Impulse, of course, is a quality of many hues. There can be the impulse to seduce, but it is different. It comes on as the body juices fulminate in a carnal reverie: I want that person *now*. Members of the Mile-High Club, those exclusive veterans of sex aboard 747s and DC-10s of the world's airlines, are illustrative of this genre. A brief acquaintance struck as the cocktail wagon rolls down the aisle turns into the mixed pleasure of fast, awkward sex over the chemical toilet or under a blanket, which is always just a little too skimpy. Later, just the memory of a quick thrill as one stands in line to fill out a missing baggage claim. No wooing, only an impulse to outwit the airline and its earphone fee with a cheaper, more exotic entertainment.

The real place to look for the difference between impulse in seduction and in wooing, however, is in the gestures that they prompt. An impulsive wooing gesture has—metaphorically speaking—a little more body to it.

ELEMENT 3 · ·

Beauty

Behold, you are beautiful, my love
Behold, you are beautiful
Your eyes are doves
Your lips like scarlet thread
Your breasts are like two fawns,
Twins of a gazelle
That feed among the lilies.

Your rounded thighs are like jewels,
The work of a master hand.
Your navel is a rounded bowl
That never lacks mixed wine.
Your belly is a heap of wheat
Set about with lilies.

Old Testament,
The Song of Songs

With a discussion of beauty we are lobbed straight into the domain of advertising and its corresponding pages in beauty magazines. These wicked people strip us of security and cast us into a forlorn state because the perfection seen there remains illusive. "My breasts are too small," "My nose is too big," "I am getting wrinkles," "I am going bald."

These are comparative statements generated by seeing models of supposed perfection everywhere—on TV, in movies, ads, book-jacket illustrations. A vast beauty industry urges us to make ourselves up so that we come closer to their manufactured ideal, and artists and film directors fall for it. But how ridiculous this is! Not only is it at least a little weird to turn auburn hair to black, or vice versa, but what is gained by changing brown eyes to blue with tinted contact lenses? Wearing elevated shoes? And by what right do these harpies tell *us* what is perfection? Fifteen years ago they brought in Twiggy. Then they shifted to a bustier ideal, as a result of which some women had foam shot into their breasts, to bring them closer to conformity. A few years later, the slim image of the jogger became the new ideal, and women labored to reduce their weight.

When Bo Derek's naked torso was featured full color on a 1981 calendar, many a man sighed with wistful longing. Personally, I think Bo Derek's breasts are absolutely beautiful; but that does not make them the *only* beautiful breasts. As the braless age revealed very pleasantly, there are millions of beautiful women with beautiful breasts, as distinctive and wonderful as the wines of France.

These self-doubting questions about beauty should be struck down. Rare is the person of whom it can be said (as did the Roman pundit Martial):

Why do I not kiss you, Philoenis? You are bald, you are carrotty, you are one-eyed. He who kisses you sins against nature.

John Merrick (the Elephant Man), possibly the ugliest man who ever lived, was loved by a woman. Loved because she found his spirit naive and beautiful.

Who is perfect? No one. A beautiful actress in silent films lost her stardom with the advent of talking movies because she had a squeaky, nasal voice. Her image was destroyed. Even Adonis, staggering beauty of a man, turned out to be very unbeautiful as a person. Despite Venus's seductive behavior, Adonis remained unmoved, preferring to bask in admiration of himself.

> The Maiden:
> " 'Fondling,' she saith, 'since I have hemm'd thee here
> Within the circuit of this ivory pale,
> I'll be a park, and thou shalt be my deer;
> Feed where thou wilt, on mountain or in dale;
> Graze on my lips, and if those hills be dry,
> Stray lower, where the pleasant fountains lie.' "
> Adonis:
> "Fie! No more of love;
> The sun doth burn my face; I must remove."
> Shakespeare,
> Venus and Adonis

How do looks come into wooing, as they obviously do? What happens in marriage? Why is it that at some moment the other person suddenly appears less beautiful than one had thought? It is because beauty truly is in the eye of the beholder. How is it that two people who do not have good looks can woo with great intensity, but that something about their countenances becomes unsatisfactory at a later date? Precisely the same condition will occur between two people who *are* good-looking. They do not look as good because the quality of the love has changed.

Looks are subjective, but they also are affected in *fact* by the perception of the looker. Love is radiant. The reason one doesn't do more to maintain or improve his or her looks may be because the other does not find him or her beautiful. It is a question of encouragement. The quality of one's looks is powerfully influenced by the attitude toward them. If someone says to a woman, "You are beautiful," she will feel beautiful and so become more beautiful. It is a fallacious notion that if you compliment someone it will lead him or her to become slovenly or grow lazy about appearance. Said a friend, "There is nothing that makes me feel better about myself and therefore more willing to put more into myself, than having my husband tell me I look beautiful. He did that recently, and it made me want to become more beautiful. On the other hand, if he had said, 'You're getting a bit paunchy,' that would *not* have made me want to go on a diet. Quite the opposite. It is a natural reaction. Nothing succeeds like success."

At its most fundamental level this question of beauty is resolved by the relationship. (See "The Center of Wooing," page 97.) At a more individual and prosaic level, it should be obvious that no one owns perfection; in fact part of an individual's beauty may be composed of the integration of imperfect elements. Actors and actresses often ask directors to accent their "good side" in profiles, but this is a silly conceit. It is the total aura of the physiognomy, and the sparkle and charisma that it exudes, that determines their beauty. The same is true for less celebrated mortals:

> *Is the creature too imperfect, say?*
> *Would you mend it*
> *And so end it?*

· · •

Beauty, an Example: In both real life and fiction there are countless demonstrations that beauty should not be measured by the skin-deep apparition of "looks." The meeting and subsequent love affair of Henri Gaudier and Sophie Suzanne Brzeska offers a lovely lesson in the variations of beauty.

The young man and the woman twice his age noticed each other in a reading room in Paris over a period of days. But she decided to give herself to a Russian scholar who'd also looked at her and returned her smiles. Gradually, however, she found that she was unwilling to permit the Russian more than a prolonged game of flirtation with her, and Gaudier, the young man, began to find a way to sit beside her at the table where she read. One day she asked to see his folio of drawings, and later he asked if she would consent to have him walk with her back to her lodgings. On the way he told her that he had been looking at her for many days and found her *beautiful*. This filled her with surprise, for since her childhood she had always been considered ugly, and no one had ever expressed such a thought to her before.

"Sometimes you look as if all the devils in hell possessed you," he continued.

"Then aren't you frightened of me?" she asked.

"On the contrary, I hate those mincing beauties whose expressions never change—they are no more than mummies."

They agreed to meet the next day at the Louvre and thus began a love that meant, for Gaudier, a period of years in which he sculpted with demonic intensity and energy. Both Gaudier and Brzeska were destined to die as violently as they had lived: she in a madhouse and he in the trenches of World War I. But in the brief five years of their life together he was able to produce a body of work of astonishing brilliance and originality, about which Henry Moore, the English sculptor, wrote: "He made me feel certain that in seeking to create along paths other than those of traditional sculpture it was possible to achieve beauty; since he had succeeded."

It is a comment that would not have been spoken without the beautiful Sophie Brzeska.

ELEMENT 4 · · ·

Taking Time

Had we but world enough, and time,
This coyness, lady, were no crime.

· · · · · · · · · · ·

An hundred years should go to praise
Thine eyes, and on thy forehead gaze;
Two hundred to adore each breast,
But thirty thousand to the rest;
An age at least to every part,
And the last age should show your heart.
For, lady, you deserve this state,
Nor would I love at lower rate.
  But at my back I always hear
Time's winged chariot hurrying near;
And yonder all before us lie
Deserts of vast eternity.

. . . .

Thus, though we cannot make our sun
Stand still, yet we will make him run.

Andrew Marvell,
"To His Coy Mistress"

Time is a grand thing to be generous with.

Time is something to be given. It takes other qualities unto itself. When we are enjoying a book we read slowly. We may daydream. In a daydream we not only control what happens, we control the speed with which it happens. In our daydreams we inch forward in a languorous way through a beautiful story. We run the picture more slowly than in real life.

Wooing is real life, but we can bring to it the same sweet sweep of timelessness we give to daydreams. In practical matters we try to be efficient, to save time, but in wooing we should give breadth to the possibilities of time; allow it the richness of dream time. When the sweep of the landscape is grand, then the prairie may catch afire.

ELEMENT 5 · ·

Attention

"Oh, he didn't forget. My wedding bouquet," says Bianca in Cole Porter's *Kiss Me Kate* on her anniversary. Again, his is a matter of a little, symbolical thing. The person who plows through a telephone conversation and fails to note or comment "You sound as if you have a cold" is not paying attention.

"Jack never notices what I'm wearing," a woman once remarked sadly to me. She might have been speaking for thousands of women. Notice of what someone is wearing is not crucial. Jack may be a wonderful, loving person, and may woo her in many other ways; but the fact that he doesn't notice is a small signal of inattention. If just for once one evening Jack did notice and could say "That's a pretty dress," or "I love your dress," or could honestly blurt out "You look just terrific tonight," that would be wooing. When we give someone a present we expect them, upon opening it, to say it is wonderful, beautiful, whatever. When two people who care about each other are going out for an evening, each usually spends time to select and put on clothes and perhaps adornments that they think will please the other person. That, too, is a present and can be acknowledged.

One of the chief reasons that wooing withers in a long-term relationship is that the individuals begin to take each other for granted. This is another way of saying that they stop paying attention. It is natural, perhaps, but not inevitable. In the earlier stages of wooing it is selfish and inexcusable.

One form of attention is flattery. A word of caution is in order here. There is nothing wrong with flattery per se, and the recipient may blush with pleasure. However, flattery is a minefield: if the person flattered does not believe that the words are truly meant, the effect is destroyed and the aura of sincerity the speaker cultivates may explode. Flattery is more appropriate to flirtation, which is filled with verbal fencing and hyperbole, than it is to wooing. Of course, we all want notice of our special qualities and talents, but the notice is better spoken from the heart—a blurt of pleasure that is out before the speaker knows what he has said. Too often flattery is only a verbal flourish: a sleek limousine rented for the occasion and *looking* rented, even smelling slightly of a former occupant's cigar smoke.

ELEMENT 6 · ·

Flirtation

Among many animals, as well as among humans, there is a likelihood that a new sexual partner will incite greater sexual drive and activity. This is especially true in the case of the male of the species and has become known as the Coolidge Effect from the following anecdote about our former president quoted in Donald Symons' *The Origin of Human Sexuality*.

One day the President and Mrs. Coolidge were visiting a government farm. Soon after their arrival they were taken off on separate tours. When Mrs. Coolidge passed the chicken pens she paused to ask the man in charge if the rooster copulates more than once each day. "Dozens of times," was the reply. "Please tell that to the President," Mrs. Coolidge requested. When the President passed the pens and was told about the rooster, he asked, "Same hen every time?" "Oh no, Mr. President, a different one each time." The President nodded slowly, then said, "Tell that to Mrs. Coolidge."

Thus the possibility of a new mate will provide a burst of passion and frenzy that may have slackened in a long-term relationship. It is one of the reasons why promiscuity endures even in societies that deal harshly with it. But there is another reason, according to anthropologists. Although human beings form pair-bonds of lengthy duration, they are not, like some other animals, likely to restrict themselves to just one bond, and may in the course of a life have several.

Whether this is right or wrong, it is a fact, and a great deal of flirtation takes place between people who are otherwise already committed.

A young girl sits plucking petals from a daisy: "He loves me, he loves me not, he loves me . . ." She goes on, hoping that the last petal will sustain her wish. The same routine in French has a richer possibility: "*Il m'aime: un peu, à la folie, passionnément, pas du tout*" (He loves me: a little, for fun, passionately, not at all).

In the adult world there is a metaphoric daisy lurking in every encounter: the Coolidge Effect. It is the genesis of flirtation.

"I like you," the man says to a young woman, or, in the manner of flirtation, something more exaggerated. She wants to believe that he means the words, and she carries the memory of them with her. She is married; he is not (or is). It is a flirtation. But when they are in the same room together, accidentally, at a party, he remembers her, and she what he has said. Out of a bustle of people they come together in a group of two and talk. They talk without guilt or passion, but as they pass the time each is basking in the pleasure of the other's presence, and gradually the flirtatious gambits will be replaced with more honest conversation.

The outcome is not predictable. What started as flirtation can take one of many courses. In a melodrama the couple would meet again—this time clandestinely—and start to speak of passion. In the love magazines, of course, declarations of eternal attachments would be traded, and after painful confrontations with existing lovers, they would walk off, not into muted moonglow but into radiant sun.

It happens every day, this tentative but loaded attraction. Neither initially sought out the other, but once found a bond was formed.

What happens next cannot be dictated by any counsel. The dart, with just a hint of curare, has struck. What happens will happen and will be as var-

ied as the diverse narratives of the eternal triangle described by the bards.

ELEMENT 7 · · ·
Throwaway Wooing

A man enters the subway, passes through the turn-
stile and starts down the staircase. He notices a woman proceeding in the same direction. He continues to
notice her as they stand on the platform awaiting the
train. She is attractive, and she is also noticing him.
The train rolls in and they get on. He sits down, as
does she, across the aisle some distance down the car
from him.

During the ride and through the next few stops
they look at each other, not constantly but almost
systematically from time to time. The train reaches
Times Square, and the woman stands up and starts to
make her way to the exit. As she passes the man she
drops a note in his lap. He picks it up, opens it, and
reads: "What would life be without fantasies?" The
woman leaves the car and the door closes behind her.

Throwaway wooing.

There was no context for the wooing, and so there
is nothing more to the story (although the man spent
the next few months obsessed by the incident). Nev-
ertheless, throwaway wooing is very different from
flirtation. Sincerity is present, even if the moment is
brief and has no consequences. The culture of the
United States does not encourage throwaway woo-

ing, perhaps because we are guarded in our expressions of many things we feel. France, for example, is very different in these matters. Frenchmen delight in using a snatch of time to delve into the life of a stranger. They are curious, interested people, respectful of women they have not met before and may never see again. It is not that they are making a pass at the woman, although that may happen. They want to *know* the woman, and in the animation of a brief conversation they are happy to reveal themselves.

A different story. A young actress is invited to a theater party. The room is filled with celebrities and she feels out of place, awkward. A young man notices her from across the room and weaves his way through the crowd to her. He has a handful of peanuts from which he has been nibbling. He opens her hand and pours a few peanuts into it. "I only wish they were emeralds" are his first words to her. It could have been throwaway wooing, but it was not: her name was Helen Hayes; his, Charles MacArthur. Thus began their long, loving relationship. There was context. It was not throwaway wooing.

ELEMENT 8 · ·

Messages

Hamlet:
To the celestial, and my soul's idol, the most beautiful
Ophelia—

. . . . .

Doubt thou the stars are fire;
  Doubt that the sun doth move;
Doubt truth to be a liar;
  But never doubt I love.

. . . .

I have not art to reckon my groans; but that I love thee
best,
O most best! Believe it. Adieu. . . .

Shakespeare,
Hamlet

We live in the electronic age; it is not surprising that the written word has ceased to be an important means of wooing. For special occasions there are printed cards. We telegraph flowers and a clerk takes the ball-point pen he has just addressed the package with and writes on a card: *Love from Jim.* The woman gets the flowers and calls Jim on the phone to say thanks. It is a cold operation from start to finish. If Jim had picked the flowers and brought them to her it would have been powerful wooing. Lacking a garden and proximity, there was still a better option. He could have written a letter. He could have had the florist send it with the flowers; or the letter could have been mailed all by itself. *One letter is worth a thousand roses.*

Letters are stronger than words spoken. They are concrete and permanent and their messages can be read and read again. Also, since we usually read a letter more slowly than we hear words in speech, there is the opportunity to savor nuance, reflect on emotion. A one-sentence paragraph, "I love you," in the middle of a letter has a powerful effect, far more stirring than if spoken, because, sadly, as D. H. Lawrence pointed out, "I love you" from the lips may be something of a motto, or cliché.

Young women used to keep the letters they received from wooers in special corners of bureau drawers, opening them periodically to relive their responses to golden messages. And in many a family attic a younger generation, cleaning out the ephemera of yesterday, has come across a packet of yellowed envelopes carefully tied in a faded pink ribbon, the paper brittle with age but the words clear and potent enough still to bring tears.

Letter writing merits a renaissance. It takes longer than a phone call but has greater longevity. And often the writer, who has time to frame his thoughts or hers, sends an expression of love that would never have come in ordinary parlance.

Is this an absurd suggestion, an anachronism? ("I got your letter. Why didn't you call?") No more so than is a return to wooing itself. We want to be noticed, remembered, thought of, courted. We yearn for the attention of the person we care for. A letter is the avowal of that. It lasts far longer and says more than any hybrid pink carnation.

For more than twenty years Bernard Shaw wooed the actress Ellen Terry, and she him, through a correspondence. They met but once. It certainly was not a typical courtship even for its day. In fact, it could be said to be unique. However, their ardor was not diminished by the fact that it was expressed in letters. Shaw, compiling the correspondence for publication years later, wrote in his introductory commentary:

Let those who may complain that it was all on paper remember that only on paper has humanity yet achieved glory, beauty, truth, knowledge, virtue, and abiding love.

Letter writing has never been perceived as an easy, automatic skill. Committing an emotional thought to paper can create sufficient trepidation to freeze the ink. A hundred years ago Webster published a handy guide to help the would-be suitor-by-mail. It was entitled: *Webster's Ready-made Love Letters Comprising Every Style and Kind of Note and Letter Upon Every Imaginable Occasion From the Very First Acquaintance Until Marriage, From Ladies to Gentlemen, and From Gentlemen to Ladies, With Full Details of the Customs and Etiquette of Courtship and Marriage, to Which is Added a Complete Directory of Poetical Quotations Related to Love, Courtship, and Marriage.* It is quite a wonderful collection. The letters need only be copied and the blanks filled in with names and occasional particulars.

Some categories: From a Gentleman to a Lady whom he has met Casually; Favorable answer to the Foregoing; Unfavorable answer to the Foregoing; From a Gentleman Accusing his Love of Flirting; to a Gentleman who has Sent an Absurdly Romantic Love Letter; From A Western Man Who Has Volunteered to Fight the Indians (which concludes: "Goodbye, goodbye, God Bless you. Be kind to my poor old gray-haired mother. If I return, it will be all right in this world; if I don't return, we will meet in heaven").

The book concludes with a series of tempestuous declarations. Unlike the other letters in the collection, which are meant to be used *verbatim,* these are samples from which a letter writer is encouraged to excerpt appropriate passages. The letters postulate a period of time during which the loved ones are apart. The first letter of the series reads:

FROM E____F____, ESQ., TO E____M____.
                                    ____Hotel, London.

For the first time in my life I write to you! How my hand trembles—how my cheek flushes! a thousand thousand thoughts rush upon me, and almost suffocate me with the variety and confusion of the emotions they awaken! I am agitated alike with the rapture of writing to you, and with the impossibility of expressing the feelings which I cannot distinctly unravel even to myself. You love me, Emily, and yet I have fled from you, and at your command; but the thought that, though absent, I am not forgotten, supports me through all.

It was with a feverish sense of weariness and pain that I found myself entering this vast reservoir of human vices. I became at once sensible of the sterility of that polluted soil so incapable of nurturing affection, and I clasped your image the closer to my heart. It is you who, when I was most weary of existence, gifted me with a new life. You breathed into me a part of your own spirit; my soul feels that influence, and becomes more sacred. I have shut myself from the idlers who would molest me;

I have built a temple in my heart; I have set within it a divinity; and the vanities of the world shall not profane the spot which has been consecrated to *you*. Our parting, Emily—do you recall it? Your hand clasped in mine, your cheek resting, though but for an instant, on my bosom; and the tears which love called forth, but which virtue purified even at their source. Never were hearts so near, yet so divided; never was there an hour so tender, yet so unaccompanied with danger. Passion, grief, madness, all sank beneath your voice, and lay hushed like a deep sea within my soul!

I tore myself from you; I hurried through the wood; I stood by the lake, on whose banks I had often wandered with you; I bared my breast to the winds; I bathed my temples with the waters. Fool that I was! the fever, the fever was within! But it is not thus, my adored and beautiful friend, that I should console and support you. Even as I write, passion melts into tenderness, and pours itself in softness over your remembrance. The virtue so gentle, yet so strong; the feelings so kind, yet so holy; the tears which wept over the decision your lips proclaimed—these are the recollections which come over me like dew. Let your own heart, my Emily, be your reward; and know that your lover only forgets that he *adores,* to remember that he *respects* you!

Reading these letters, one is almost tempted to laugh. One does laugh! At the same time, they do offer us a sense of confidence. We may be somewhat out of practice at writing letters, but the impulse and the effort is almost as natural to us as anything else in wooing. Nothing could be more instinctive than, upon feeling a surge of fondness, eroticism or the ache of missing someone, to jot down our thoughts and send them to the person causing the sensation.

No one knows how often experiences of the heart are transmitted between real people using the pre-formed texts of greeting cards. But we do not need the ready-made. *Any* letter, however brief, is its own message. The fact alone that it was written says the sender has had the recipient very much in mind. What it states is just an orchestration of that point. *One letter is worth a thousand roses.*

Still, it would slight the value of greeting cards not also to make their defense. Karen speaks of them: Her husband, she says, spends literally an hour reading the message on *every* card available in order to select the one that best expresses what he wants her to know from him. And because she knows this, she looks forward to the cards and reads very carefully the messages they contain. For her they are a painstaking and lyrical way of saying "I wish you the best for the New Year" or "I love you."

It is not a violation of language or good taste to express passion in a letter with drama, Webster's hyperboles notwithstanding. Perhaps the best example contained in a letter of a lyrical description of love's pain is Cyrano de Bergerac's final message to Roxanne:

> . . . *No more*
> *Shall my eyes drink the sight of you like wine;*
> *Never more with a look that is a kiss,*
> *Follow the sweet grace of you—*
> *I remember now the way*

You have, of pushing back a lock of hair
With one hand, from your forehead—and my heart
Cries out.

As a footnote to changing times in letters it is interesting to note the evolution of "personals" in classified advertising. Glance through an urbane publication like the *New York Review of Books* or the *Maine Times* and you will find, typically: "Middle-aged single man with interest in music and gardening seeks companionship with woman in her 40s with similar tastes." It is a broadside petition to no one in particular. Compare it with the staid but almost saucy advertisement typical of London papers in the last century (this example quoted from E. S. Turner's *History of Courting*): "A Gentleman with a Spencer Wig who marched in the first rank of the Volunteers last Tuesday was particularly taken notice of by a lady of easy fortune and who the world says has some share of beauty. If the said Gentleman is single and is disposed to send a line directed to D. B. at the Somerset Coffee House in the Strand, intimating his name and place of abode; if upon inquiry the lady finds his character answerable to his outward appearance, she will then appoint him a meeting."

ELEMENT 9 ···

Eyes

Eyes are bold as hours—roving, running, leaping. . . .
They speak all languages. What inundation of life and
thought is discharged from one soul to another through
them.

Ralph Waldo Emerson

· ·•

A group of women recently was asked to name their
favorite movie. The criterion they were asked to apply was "the most romantic." Their choices included
Gone With the Wind, Brief Encounter, Doctor Zhivago,
Romeo and Juliet. Most, however, named *Casablanca.*
There is no sex in the film, no eroticism, even. So
why? A number of reasons came out in conversation:
the exotic setting, wartime, the battle of good and
evil, epitomized by the emotional singing of the
"Marseillaise" to drown out the German voices, the
melancholy piano playing of Dooley Wilson and the
now legendary "As Time Goes By." Above all, they
spoke of the way Bogart and Bergman looked at each
other—the language of their eyes, wherein all emotions were made plain without a word: the first
searching glances of reappraisal, noncommittal; the
doubts; and then the looks that were tinted with
memories; the silent appeals and denials; pain, surrender, memory, love. Men love *Casablanca* too, and
for the same reasons. Ask any man what about Ingrid

Bergman comes to mind in a vision of the film. Bosom? Legs? Never. The answer is her *face*. And what of the face: beauty of bone and skin is part of the answer, but one universal answer is the eyes. The eyes told the story; "love's tongue is in the eyes."

A silent language is invented and transmitted through the eyes, and if a large part of wooing is the expression of feeling, then the eyes are paramount. The poets were well aware of this:

Ben Johnson:

> *Drink to me only with thine eyes,*
> *And I will pledge with mine.*

John Ford:

> *Such a pair of stars*
> *As are thine eyes would, like Prometheus' fire,*
> *If gently glanced, give life to senseless stones.*

Shakespeare, of course, is filled with eye power. Iago tried to stir jealousy in Cassio by describing Desdemona's eyes:

Cassio: She's a most exquisite lady.
Iago: And, I'll warrant her, full of game.
Cassio: Indeed, she's a most fresh and delicate creature.
Iago: What an eye she has! Methinks it sounds a parley of provocation.
Cassio: An inviting eye; and yet methinks right modest.

Elsewhere, the bard writes:

> *A lover's eyes will gaze an eagle blind; . . .*
> . . . .
> *From women's eyes this doctrine I derive:*

They sparkle still the right Promethean fire;
They are the books, the arts, the academes,
That show, contain, and nourish all the world.

And, *"Her eyes have shot their arrows into my heart."*

And Cyrano's heartbreaking:

Nevermore, with a look that is a kiss
Follow the sweet grace of you.

"The eyes tell all," and "the eyes don't lie" are common expressions. The makeup of some people is such that their eyes have a power to dominate other people. Robert Kennedy had such eyes, and Rasputin reportedly did. All of us can use our eyes both to send our messages and to read their answers in other eyes. A politician shaking hands with morning commuters at a subway entrance knows that if he looks into their eyes, he'll be remembered. Auto salesmen can tell when they have named an acceptable price by a giveaway look in a customer's eyes, and a cardplayer knows that the hardest part of maintaining a poker face is controlling his eyes.

In wooing, the eyes telegraph the progressional phases: recognition, appraisal, salutation, warmth, desire, acceptance. "The emoting eye" has been neglected in the Age of Concupiscence. Even though women spend time and money on makeup for their eyes, this has been an effort to enhance beauty, not necessarily expressiveness. Now, with a return to the art of wooing, a renaissance of the eyes is at hand. In courtship they will show tenderness, lust, reserve, abandon, coquetry, rapture. They will communicate a blush, a refusal, a question. They will show pleasure and delight and make the subtle distinction between the two. Perhaps better than many spoken expressions, they will speak of yearning, of love: ". . . and she looked at him with such a profound longing that he was compelled to . . ." It is fascinating, the many, many ways the eyes have of communicating. Once one is alert to their potential, a whole tapestry of signals can be recognized and sent through them.

For a shy person the eyes are a way around words.

In a flirtation, the eyes play a fast game, sparkling with impudence, widening with affected surprise. They will signal roguish come-ons and then contradict themselves with a visible toss of the head. At one moment they may say, "Hello, you big hunk of handsome man"; at the next they will feign incognizance.

Aside from direct espousal, eye to eye, there are a multitude of other ways in which eyes speak. Eyes that are meeting eyes and suddenly turn away to follow another person walking into a room may not cause jealousy but do break the spell; they cause the owner of the other set of eyes an instant of unsettlement, of doubt.

There are eyes that bore in. This happens when eyes are not looking at another's eyes but through them, into the deep center of what lies behind them. This can be disconcerting, is always intense, and often is a way of questioning the truth of words coming from the lips. "Looking daggers" at someone is a variant of this. And it takes only a second or two for a man's eyes to leave a woman's and brush down her neck and across her breasts. Yet that flicker is sufficient to cause a blush.

One woman describes how she met the man she lives with. She was at a convention dinner, sitting at one of those big round tables that companies take for their employees and special clients. She was seated between two men. Next to the man on her right sat another woman, then another man. At one point during the meal she looked over in the general direction of this second man. He was talking with someone across the table, but without moving his head his eyes moved quietly to her, and then he was looking right into her eyes out of the corners of his. There is something unusually powerful about a clear, directed gaze that comes from the corners of the eyes. She glanced in his direction frequently. He seemed always to feel it and would look at her in that way. She decided to try it herself. With her head held forward toward the center of the table, while playing with her place card, she listened pensively to the man on her left, nodding a little; then she turned her eyes to the right and looked at the man with a penetrating gaze. He turned toward her and their eyes met, and for the rest of the meal and during the speeches they kept meeting each other's eyes in the sidelong glance. "It was direct and left a very strong sensation," she says. It was so strong, in fact, that when finally everyone was free to get up and move to the open bar he and she headed straight toward each other, met and started talking. They're *still* talking.

There is no way to rehearse the language of the eyes, although actors and actresses preparing to play a part do rehearse. For the most part, there's no need. Our eyes respond automatically to the thoughts behind them. It is only to use them.

An aside on eyeglasses: Gloria's story.

Gloria settled down into her assigned seat on an airplane. She was looking forward to the trip immensely. Although it was primarily a business trip, the work awaiting her was simple and brief. Behind her lay all the confusion of responsibilities, phones, orders, clients.

She stretched luxuriantly and closed her eyes as the plane took off. Soon the stewardess came with the cocktail wagon. The man sitting next to her ordered a drink and so did she. He was attractive—probably in his mid-forties, with a little gray in his hair at the temples. He was reading a business report until his drink was served; then he put aside the report, took off his reading glasses and enjoyed the cocktail.

"Going to Dallas?" he asked her. She answered yes. They talked about Texas; it was easy, pleasant talk, and before long the conversation was ranging among a variety of mutual interests. Gloria thought it would be nice to have dinner in Dallas with this man and wondered whether he'd suggest it—but then, to her chagrin, he reached into his breast pocket, withdrew his reading glasses and put them on.

"I was a confused 'wooee,' " she stated some days later. The moment the man restored his glasses it was an unequivocal signal that the affair had ended and practical matters were again at hand.

Until I heard this story it hadn't occurred to me that there is an eyeglass etiquette in wooing. But it provokes a thought: that there is a direct body language involved with glasses. To take them off, put them away (in the case of the reading variety), is a way of saying hello. When this is done by a person with a more serious visual impairment it can mean one of two things. Vanity: I think I am more attractive if I remove them; or more simply, I don't need them. (Rarely: With this lemon better to be myopic.) Again, when the glasses go on, does it mean I am what I am, or I want to be able to see this lady?

Many people are self-conscious about glasses, probably because in the beauty ads no one wears them. Yet they do not impair the beauty of the wearer; in fact, they are often attractive. When my wife and I first knew each other she always kept her glasses off. Without glasses her face was very beautiful. But suffering from nearsightedness, she says, she never could be certain of the expression on my face, which was awkward for her. I still think she is beautiful without glasses, but love her no less with them on. And am happy that she can see me.

ELEMENT 10 · ·

The Grand Gesture

The courtship of the white-fronted dectic is short, a
bit bizarre, and not a little poignant. The following
description was written by Remy de Gourmont and
translated by Ezra Pound.

The white-fronted dectic is, like all the Locustians
(grasshoppers), a very ancient insect; it existed in
the coal era, and it is perhaps this antiquity which
explains its peculiar fecundative method. As the
cephalopodes, his contemporaries, he has recourse
to the spermatophore; yet there is mating, there is
embracing; there are play and caresses. Here are the
couple face to face, they caress each other with long
antennae "fine as hair" . . . after a moment they
separate. The next day, new encounter, new blan-
dishments. Another day . . . finds the male
knocked down by the female, who overwhelms
him with her embrace; he gnaws her belly. The
male disentangles himself and escapes, but a new
assault masters him, he lies flat on his back. This
time the female, lifted on her high legs, holds him
belly to belly; she bends back the extremity of her
abdomen; the victim does likewise, there is junc-
tion, and soon one sees something enormous issue
from the convulsive flanks of the male, as if the animal were pushing out its entrails. "It is," continues
the best observer . . . "an opaline leather bottle
about the size and colour of a mistletoe berry," a
bottle with four pockets at least, held together by
feeble sutures. The female receives the leather bot-

tle, or spermatophore, and carries it off glued to her belly. Having got over the thunderclap, the male gets up, makes his toilet; the female browses as she walks. "From time to time she rises on her stilts, bends into a ring, seizes her opaline bundle in her mandibles, and chews it gently." She breaks off little pieces, chews them carefully, and swallows them. Thus while the fecundative particles are stravastated toward the eggs which they are to animate, the female devours the spermatic pouch. After having tasted it piece by piece she suddenly pulls it off, kneads it, swallows it whole. Not a scrap is lost; the place is clear, and the oviscapte is cleaned, washed, polished. The male has begun to sing again, during this meal, but it is not a love-song, he is about to die; he dies: passing near him at this moment, the female looks at him, smells him, takes a bite out of his thigh.

Wooing does not require a mortal gesture. Nor does it require diamond pendants and dinners for a week at "21." When Walter Raleigh threw his cloak over a puddle to keep a lady's feet dry he was making a grand gesture. Ulrich, chopping off his finger, was making a grand (and perhaps lunatic) gesture. Cheshire cheese became a grand gesture; so did Doug's small advertisement in the *New York Times*. Little things can be grand gestures.

Perhaps Sir Walter Raleigh's cloak and the Cheshire cheese could be called elements of courtesy. But they are also something more than that. Courtesy is a form of manners, and manners are set, prescribed. Thus, if they were *only* acts of courtesy, one could say that they were only matters of duty as defined by social convention. The grand gesture, however, goes beyond any expectation: it is an act done impulsively, and the impulse comes not from a desire to conform but to do, or please.

And Liv Ullmann describes a grand (and extravagant) gesture. She is out with a man who is new in her life. During dinner a messenger arrives with a package for the man. He hands it to her. "I had it flown from the coast today," he tells her. She opens it. Inside is a diamond bracelet. She is abashed by the opulence of the gift. But then there is more: he tells her that he has had the bracelet for years, even before his marriage. He says that the reason he bought it was that it was so beautiful he felt the instant he saw it that "this will be for the woman of my life." And so she is being told that with all the women he has known and even during his three marriages he has never given it away; and after one dinner with her, he has it flown from California. "I was a helpless victim," she recalls.

A man I know saw a lovely woman sitting with a friend of his at a Chinese restaurant. This man went to the kitchen and wrote a little note saying *The man opposite you is going to be the man of your life,* and he had the cook put it into a fortune cookie. Then he went to the table of his friend, said hello, and sat down opposite the woman. The fortune cookies were brought in; when she opened hers, he had won her. The fantastical element beneath the ruse was very effective.

The presentation of the diamond bracelet was certainly a grand gesture. One wonders, however, how often it was employed by the man in question: one almost imagines a drawer full of diamond bracelets awaiting their targets. If there is calculation in the gesture it may still serve wooing; however, simple and uncalculated gestures will be equally appreciated.

Often in gestures, as with many things, less is more.

· · •

A grand gesture can be unabashedly romantic; for me, this is epitomized in the story of Martha, who performs the ultimate act of female wooing in the opera of the same name, by Friedrich von Flotow.

Lady Harriet Durham (Martha) is part of a bored nobility. For diversion she and a friend decide to dress up in peasant clothes and go to the Richmond Fair, which, among other things, is the place where servants are hired. Much to their horror the two ladies find that they have been selected by a pair of bumpkins, Lionel and Plunkett, to keep house for them. The sheriff informs them that their contract is binding for one year. At Lionel's and Plunkett's farmhouse, the men put the girls to work—even teach them how to spin wool, something they have never done in their heretofore privileged lives. Lionel becomes smitten by Martha. He asks her to sing him a song, and she complies with the melancholy "Last Rose of Summer." Lionel, now in a fit of love, asks Martha to marry him. Martha laughs at him but is touched by his devotion.

That night the girls decide it is high time to make their escape, and they do. A few days later Lionel, who is walking despondently through the woods, lamenting his lost love, hears the sounds of an approaching hunting party—which includes Martha, now restored to the normal attire of Lady Harriet Durham. Before seeing Lionel she sings fondly of her memory of him. He recognizes her, runs up to her, and speaks his love. She denies that she is Martha, which incenses him; soon he tells the assembled courtiers of Martha's contract to him as a servant. She feigns ignorance and states he must be mad. Poor Lionel is tied up and taken away, presumed to be a lunatic.

Then, in one of those marvelous *dei ex machina* of opera, Lionel remembers a ring he was given by his dying father, with the instruction that if he is ever in dire trouble he should send it to the queen. Matters are straightened out; the ring establishes that he is of noble birth, and Lady Harriet—Martha—asks him to marry her. By now, however, his love has been twisted into scorn, and he leaves her in fury.

What to do? Martha embarks on a grand gesture. She decides to convert Plunkett's farmyard into a replica of the fairground at Richmond. Lionel arrives there with his friend, and when the bell rings, signaling the time for the hiring of servants, Lady Harriet suddenly appears, dressed once again as Martha, and has herself sold to Lionel. He, certain from this romantic, self-humbling act that she does truly love him, sweeps her into his arms, and the opera ends as they sing "The Last Rose of Summer" in duet.

ELEMENT 11 · ·

Sex

This is not a book about sex, but if wooing includes elements of respect, spontaneity, simplicity, expressiveness, then it is logical to include sex as an extension of wooing.

There is a baby born every second on this planet. That means that every second thousands of people are completing the sex act. Just about all of them are accomplishing this without benefit of the current spate of sex "how-to" books (say, 100,000,000 sex acts each day, versus just a relative handful of books). Yet there are enough of these books in print in the United States to fill a small library. They range from the basic prescriptions of arousal and intercourse to descriptions of complex and bizarre variations on sexual pleasure. It can be argued that this literature has served some useful purposes and has had at least one negative effect.

On the positive side, the very existence of these books has opened up—legitimated—the discussion of sex. We no longer feel we need to mail away covertly for a book that will arrive in a plain brown wrapper and read it furtively in solitary moments. We can talk about sex and explore the infinite varieties of sexual pleasure that it once seemed deviant even to consider. Taking sex out of the closet has been beneficial; after all, for the human species, procreation is the least frequent reason why we have intercourse. Pleasure is the primary reason. Our pleasure may be of many types: local, general, emotional, etc., from the physically thrilling release of the orgasmic contraction to the sublime moment of an embrace between two lovers whose rapture is experienced in each of the thousand places where their bodies touch.

The sex-tech books probably do not have much effect at such moments, but at least they liberated the knowledge that it is all right to have such encounters on the floor, in a field, morning or afternoon, in light as well as in darkness.

A second salutary effect of these books is that they have given men and women an intensive course in the female orgasm. It is generally agreed among biologists and zoologists that the human species is unique in the animal world in this respect: no other female, even among the primates, experiences orgasm. Yet just because women are physically equipped for orgasm does not mean they will automatically experience it during intercourse. In certain societies the potential for the female orgasm is *unknown*. Forms of foreplay and copulation in these societies are such that there is inadequate time for the female to achieve orgasm, although she may enjoy the act of intercourse. On this point Margaret Mead wrote: "Comparative cultural material gives no grounds for assuming that an orgasm is an integral and unlearned part of women's sexual response, as it is of men's sexual response, and strongly suggests that a greater part of women's copulatory behavior is *learned*" (emphasis added).

As an example of this, Donald Symons writes:

Consider Marshall's data on sexual behavior on Mangaia, a southern Cook Island in central Polynesia, where all women are said to orgasm during intercourse. At the age of thirteen or fourteen Mangaian boys undergo superincision [circumcision] and at this time are instructed in sexual matters by the superincision expert. The expert emphasizes techniques of coitus, cunnilingus, kissing and sucking the breasts, and bringing the partner to several orgasms before the male allows himself to ejaculate. According to Marshall, Mangaian knowledge of sexual anatomy probably is more extensive than that of most European physicians. Two weeks after superincision there is a "practice exercise" in intercourse with an older, experienced woman. She coaches the neophyte in applying the information he has acquired from the superincision expert, especially the techniques of delaying and timing ejaculations so that he orgasms simultaneously with his partner.

Girls of the same age are instructed in sexual matters by an older woman. Although sexual intercourse in Mangaia typically is preceded by only about five minutes of foreplay, Marshall emphasizes that considerable skill is applied during those five minutes; Mangaians are not interested in foreplay for its own sake, and the only goal is to arouse the female sufficiently for intercourse. To Mangaians, extended foreplay detracts from their primary goal which is fifteen to thirty minutes of intercourse with continuous thrusting and active female participation, during which the female orgasms two or three times, her final orgasm occurring simultaneously with her partner's. Mangaians state that orgasm must be "learned" by a woman and that this learning process is achieved through the efforts of a good man (from *Origin of Human Sexuality*).

Thus the sex-tech books and the research a few of them embody serve as a kind of Western shaman in matters of the female orgasm. Perhaps as we as a society become able to talk more freely of sexual sensations and desires, the books will become redundant. Men will learn from women and vice versa.

Yet "helpful hints" is a phrase that must be applied with some care. Some of the advice in the sex-tech books is ridiculous at best and absolutely wrong at worst. Consider this counsel in *How to Make Love to a Single Girl* by Rober M., under the heading "Tell Her You Love Her Vagina": ". . . do a chick a favor. Tell her her pussy is far-out. Tell her it's the most beautiful snatch you ever saw. . . ." I am not aware of the evidence for a positive response upon which the author based his suggestion, but among the respondents to *this* book it was about the last thing they hoped to hear.

For all their "helpful hints," these books do create a different and enormous problem. With their endless commentary on sexual performance, they exacerbate all sorts of residual insecurities. Having made a fetish of supreme performance, the books then intend to guide a reader to infallibility. But that is impossible. There will always be times of better and worse sex—even orgasms differ in their intensity. Making love may be so intense an emotional experience that the physical climax is almost an anticlimax. There are times of sheer sexual abandon in wooing as well.

An example: "I sucked her furiously—her body was covered with sweat—and she was tired after dancing—she was cold—I covered her with my pe-lisse, and she fell asleep with her fingers in mine. As for me, I scarcely shut my eyes. Watching that beautiful creature asleep (she snored, her head against my arm: I had slipped my forefinger under her necklace), my night was one long, infinitely intense reverie. . . . As for the *coups,* they were good—the third especially was ferocious, and the last tender—we told each other many sweet things—toward the end there was something sad and loving in the way we embraced." This is from Flaubert, a serious and attentive wooer, describing a night with the courtesan Kuchuk Hanem, in a letter to Louis Bouilhet, March 1850.

So it is. No sex-tech can speak of these things; and by the books' emphasis on technique they have helped to shear the greatest of all moments of the freedom that nurtures the splendor. Stendahl wrote: "Nothing is so interesting as passion; everything about it is so unexpected, and its agent is also its victim. Nothing could be duller than measured love, where everything is calculated, as in all the prosaic affairs of everyday life."

· · •

Kissing:

"Your lips suck forth my soul. See where it flies." What is kissing? It is "the anatomical juxtaposition of two orbicu-laris orbis muscles in a state of contraction." But it is also this: "A secret told to the mouth instead of to the ear."

"I kissed her on the tip av the nose an' undher the eye;

an' a girl that lets a kiss come tumbleways like that has never been kissed before. . . . That day I throd on rollin' clouds. All earth was too small to hould me. Begad I cud ha' hiked the sun out av the sky for a live' coal to my pipe, so magnificent was I" (Rudyard Kipling, *"The Courting of Dinah Shadd"*).

How dare a book attempt to explain to me what is a kiss!

· · •

The Penis: It is a sad comment on the prospect of sexual happiness for many that men have become so obsessed with the size of the penis. The fact is that the human penis is considerably larger than that bestowed upon any other primate, including the gorilla.

Of course there are differences. There are short ones, large ones, thick ones, stubby ones, smooth ones, rough ones, white ones, pink ones, black ones, gray ones. Some have knobby heads, huge heads, small heads; some have symmetry in their erection; others twist a bit right or left. In erection some aim upward, others straight; some droop a bit. Some can stay hard for long periods of time; some even after ejaculation. Some are circumcised, others not. In erection, the blood vessels bulge under the skin of some. Some, when they ejaculate, send a spurt of semen several feet. Others just exude the necessary drops. Some penises are extremely sensitive on their heads, others on the underside ridge. In others sensation is spread throughout the shaft. Some penises can reach ejaculation in just a few short strokes, others require half an hour. And the time will vary with the same penis from occasion to occasion.

What does this have to do with making love to a woman? Very little. Recall the Mangaians, who too display these varieties among their males. The elements of sexual satisfaction for a woman are not measured by centimeters of the penis. But what are the implications for a man? Unfortunately, many psychiatrists and therapists report that the emphasis on "performance" has also led to a preoccupation with penis profile. Because the penis is a man's instrument of ultimate physical pleasure it is natural to check it out to ensure it is up to the job. And that invariably leads to comparisons. Probably every man would like a bigger rather than a smaller penis because it can be an emblem of "manliness." But every man who ever masturbated as an adolescent (which is just about every man) is unaware and uncaring at the moment of orgasm just where his penis stands in the great scheme of comparison. The pleasure is there. What is important is the intensity of pleasure the penis provides its owner or a partner. However, this truth becomes obscured in postadolescent years, partly as a result of pulp magazines and pornographic literature. "What turns a woman on?" asks a typical reader's column in a men's magazine. "A huge prick" invariably shows up among the female answers. (This makes exciting copy, which is why the magazine editors, who manufacture many of these responses, drop it in.) Men, reading this, become nervous. Am I adequate? Do I turn a woman on? However, one has only to watch a few hard-core movies to realize that the heralded organ is not so different among the porn stars as among ourselves, and it seems to work pretty well no matter how it looks.

A few years ago a serious research study on healthy body size-weight proportions announced that people would be healthier if the average optimum weight were increased by approximately six to eight pounds. Suddenly many people who had been struggling to lose a last, difficult few pounds found they were *okay*. If a study were released tomorrow showing that the size of the average erect penis was five inches in 1984, men would be giggling with excitement. On the other hand, if the study found the figure to be nine inches there would be a national crisis of male security. Interest in the penis is historic: primitive and sophisticated cultures alike have paid homage to it, constructed giant phalluses of marble, wood, and other materials. Interest in, even glorification of, the phallus is not likely to evaporate. However, in the course of asking dozens of women what they hope for in a man, what would sweep them off their feet, even what they hope for when a man makes love, I never heard gargantuan genitalia given as an answer.

Subsequent chapters on wooing reveal what it is that women yearn for. If they experience that, there will be happy endings.

· · •

The Breasts, Pudenda, Etc: Obvious differences being set aside, reread the comment on the penis, substituting female external sexual parts.

. . •

Sexual Liberation: Because of the freedom to talk of, read of, and look at (in film and video) a panoply of sexual behavior, we are launched on an era of sexual liberation. There are some who argue that this is sinful or that some of the sexual antics permitted within it are unnatural. Recreational sex is criticized for devaluating emotional elements in lovemaking. But if sex among humans is not primarily a reproductive act, then why not experiment with what is sexually pleasurable, especially if you're experimenting together with someone you care for and respect? Even among other animals, for whom reproduction *is* the prime function, sexual "antics" are not uncommon. Of course when sexual license among people begins to extend into group or random sex, then the spirit of consummation of courtship is being violated, and it is no longer part of wooing.

Western society has come so quickly to sexual liberation that matters of what is permissible are still quite tentative. (After all, it was only one hundred years ago, in the Victorian era, that people avoided speaking of the "legs" of tables because the word was too close to signifying physical anatomy. Books on library shelves were carefully arranged to segregate male authors from female ones.) For some people emancipation from Victorian mores is complete, but for many it still is shaky. Still, when a man and a woman have wooed each other, there is no reason why any prescriptive limit should be placed on their exploration of a pleasure that is, after all, natural, mutual and endlessly repeatable.

Some will argue that sex is sex, but I believe there is a difference in both attitude and demeanor when sex is part of wooing. Among non-wooers, where boredom reigns or sex-tech has become a bible, sex is splintering, separating: two cold plates of steel cushioned from each other by padding; two people trying hard.

· • ●

Sex in Wooing: Among wooers it is generally true that their relationship eventually will lead to sexual union. It may lead to love or to friendship, to marriage or to none of these, but it will almost always lead to a physical desire to caress, to a craving for mutual sexual embrace. That is not to say that sex is the dominating and primary sensation of wooing. A man and woman woo each other because they find in each other qualities they enjoy and respect.

The wonderful thing about sex in wooing is that pressures created by outside oracles and umpires are removed. There is no need to qualify: questions of good and bad aren't pertinent. Obviously, there will be times when the physical pleasures of sex are more and less intense for wooers. But as sex is not the sole objective of wooing, its physical outcome is experienced very differently. Frustration, if there is any, can be resolved within a context of caring. This has proved true even when a disability has eliminated normal sex as a possibility between a couple.

It is the hour for sexual union. The hour may provide passionate reveries and lustful moments, but its best expression may be this: The body is alive and the skin is begging for a touch. The hairs on the forearm are a sensory army seeking a brushing graze. The voice is throaty, the eyes brightly intent. The head, too, is awaiting a caress. The whole epiderm seems to be an erective web of sensatory hunger. Then comes the first brush of a kiss, a touch, the stroke of a finger. Tumultuous embraces follow. The fetters of cloth impede and then are gone. And two people touch each other in what seems an infinity of places.

No two people who have wooed each other need wonder about what to do in bed. What happens will be as varied as the wooers. Sometimes there will be greedy seeking out of pleasures; at other times there will be lovemaking inside the warmth of affection. The lovemaking will be as passionate as Masters and Johnson could wish, but the way it evolves and culminates will be its own.

One account of first-time sex between a man and a woman is quoted here.

When we got back to my apartment, even though it was still quite early, we both knew that we wanted to lie down on a bed and embrace. Somehow, standing and kissing each other, saying loving things and caressing on the feet seemed awkward. The getting into bed was very uncomplicated. We simply took off our clothes, pulled back the cover, and there we were.

The first warmth of his body against mine was paralyzing in its pleasure. I did not even want to be kissing. Just to be holding each other, the warmth of skin against skin. And then to feel for the first time his hand against the bare skin of my back, my hand against his skin.

Of course, as we touched each other we soon started to move, and as we moved against each other it was electrifying. I remember saying his name and thinking how strange my voice sounded. It was so breathy—sort of like those of actresses supposedly in the throes of a climax. Yet he was not in me and had not even touched my breasts.

I don't know how long we kept on like that. Sometimes what seems like forever is in reality only an instant. But we were like that—gently moving, twining our legs, holding and caressing each other, and paralyzing each other for many minutes.

Then he touched my hair, ran his fingers behind my ear, kissed my upper lip, and I don't know why but it made me reach down and press his penis hard against my stomach. Well, I don't know all the details of how things happened after that, but eventually—we were still lying on our sides—his penis probed between my legs, and I had to have him inside me. As he slid in he made a little moan. Then again we were both paralyzed by the closeness. When we did start to move it was slowly—deep, long slow slides. I wanted to speed up, I am sure we both did, but the pleasure of not doing that was even greater. In fact, after maybe a couple of minutes of that torturous ecstasy he moved close against me, his hand holding me there, and we stopped moving. Immobile, we gave each other soft wet kisses, and all time stopped.

When it was over, I went into a sort of trance—neither awake nor asleep—and in that same loving position we lay without words and with just the softest of little touches. A sweet languor that lasted until the whole thing repeated itself. Differently, but as wonderful.

ELEMENT 12 ··

Jealousy

A strategic wooer might think that creating jealousy in the "wooee" produces some favorable results. No. Jealousy is a demon, a form of madness. Read *Othello*.

Early in this century John Jay Chapman, an undergraduate of Harvard, went to a dance. He soon noticed the girl he loved dancing with another man, which was all right. What was not all right was the *way* they were dancing and talking to each other. He tried to cut in, but the other (actually a friend) refused. Overcome by jealousy, Chapman struck the man in the face. Then, aghast at himself, he returned to college, reflected for some minutes and decided that the arm that had done such a thing was unworthy. He opened up the firebox of a coal stove and shoved the offending arm into the coals. He held it there until it was reduced to ash. For the rest of his life Chapmen walked about with one arm. Many saw what he did as a great show of honor, but if it was honor, it was honor adjudicating the consequences of jealousy.

We do not need Iago's evil construction of jealousy in *Othello*. We all know people who have been consumed by this pernicious form of madness. People commit suicide because of jealousy; commit murder. Even if a life is not taken, a life may be crippled, left with permanent scars. The person who allows jealousy to intrude in wooing—or much worse, provokes it—sins against humanity.

ELEMENT 13 · ·

Passion, Intimacy

Little boys are taught at an early age not to cry. Grown men and women in our culture stifle sorrow far more than in Latin countries, for example. Even joy, at the opposite end of the emotional spectrum, is something we express in moderation. A salesman who runs into the hall shouting "Yippee!" after landing a big order is considered somehow "immature." In these ways we are conditioned to turn our emotional responses inward.

In a similar manner we become wary of giving away too much between man and woman. Herein lies a terrible misunderstanding of opportunities in a relationship. Passion, a powerful flow of emotion, has, by its very definition, strength. The state of intimacy also makes a large statement, for it is a revelation: this is who I am.

Just as we guard against tears or the ebullient

demonstration of joy, we mask passion and ration intimacy.

With passion and intimacy, we are frightened of giving something away, and the concept of surrender is involved. Yet wooing would be much richer if the impediments to liberating passion and intimacy could be removed. I believe that can be accomplished by a simple redefinition. Instead of thinking about "giving away" something of oneself, it would be healthier and more accurate to consider it as "giving out." If I feel jubilant, feel passionate, feel longing, feel desire, I give these emotions *out*. I allow them to flow out into the air, to be noticed and received by whomever is present. There is no surrender; I have not sent these emotions away to the dry-cleaners. All I have done is to say out loud, as much to myself as anyone else, This is how I feel.

When someone has been hurt by a betrayal of trust, there will be a natural reluctance to establish a new position of vulnerability. Wooing in such instances requires a more gentle schedule, a compassionate understanding between two people. However, sooner or later the potential for a new relationship must include, once again, the giving out of the powerful elements of passion and intimacy. The reverse means cynicism, and in matters of love, cynics wither like prunes on a drying mat.

If a person is "cool" no one can turn him down because there is nothing to turn down; we do not know what is meant by, or what underlies, the coolness. However, to deny expressing passion or intimacy is to strip from wooing not only its fibre but its very soul. To emit passion and give intimacy is to liberate oneself and allow all the other elements of wooing to build a romantic universe in which two people rest and grow.

ELEMENT 14 · ·

Calculated Wooing

In the movie *Tootsie,* Dustin Hoffman, in a feminine disguise, has heard from the girl he loves what it is that would woo her. Later, in his natural male mode, he meets her at a cocktail party. She does not know him as a man. He says to her the very words—aggressive ones, admittedly—that she has said would sweep her off her feet. She throws a glass of wine in his face. His plan backfired because, although he was longing to please her, he was not wooing naturally. It was strategic and badly calculated. It was unattractive.

One cannot prescribe what the ideal wooing will be—not even the "wooee" can. Hoffman thought he had structured the perfect woo, because it came from her. However, if a woman says "the man who sends me roses . . . " she may not mean exactly this at all. It raises an enigma: don't necessarily take the woman at her word, or the man at his. Don't go by his or her formula any more than you go by someone else's.

The following comments on natural versus calculated wooing are drawn from an interview with Liv Ullmann on the subject.

"Natural wooing is recognition. It is very much recognition. It is that period before you know too much about each other, before you know what kind of life the other has and start to feel jealous about that; before you start to expect things. Wooing is simple things. It is listening or seeming to be listening; being happy just seeing the other person.

"Once you become partners wooing goes into another stage. It is no longer the initial wooing that is based on everything being new, unsaid. The moment you say, I love you, you are into something else; from then on things are starting to be expected. Why didn't he say he loved me today? Or why didn't she say, 'You are everything to me'? You're at a point where wooing will all the time be interrupted by insecurity and wondering.

"The initial wooing is just like two fishes swimming together and watching and enjoying each other.

"I think the wonderful part of wooing is when there is no pain. The best natural wooing is when you know somebody is there, happy, smiling for you, and you walk out in the sun and you just feel wonderful and everything around you is grand. You know the man is going to phone. You know you are going to meet that evening. He lets you know. That is his wooing. He lets you know that you are number one in the world. The minute you start doubting it, he is not wooing you anymore. You can maintain such a relationship for years, but it gets more complicated. Other people come in, friends, interests, things that don't go well together.

"That is the sweet way of wooing. Natural wooing. But it can happen the other way. Treat her terribly, and she will think of nothing else. Don't call her, be rough on her, suddenly leave her, and she will be your slave, hoping this is going to change. Some men do that—and women too—purposefully. Make dates with two men and have them meet at the same place, stand in a corner and laugh. That is strategic wooing. The absolutely disastrous insecurity caused by *not* calling is very effective. I have also heard of a woman leaving flowers in her flat when a man is coming, flowers from someone else; or of leaving 'by mistake' a love letter from somebody else. The man becomes frantic and woos much harder. Everything is being built on envy. And the *very* effective one is to disappear. Disappear without a trace of where you went or why you went away. Then you let him find you after a while. Calculating, strategic. It is a kind of wooing I think is only used when one is uncertain about the other person.

"Do you want the person once you have her? Wooing leads you to someone you want, but once you have that person comes the next stage: are you feeling love or were you just out for the fun of the wooing, the fun of the conquest? Many wooers just love the woo. They love being the hunter; they do not love it when the chase is over. That is when wooing stops, and reality sets in for the poor kill. Han Suyin in an interview once said something I have never forgotten. She said to women: Never tell a man you love him, because the moment you do that it is less for the man. It is inbuilt in a man to be the hunter. I do not believe that, but it was her experience. If it is true then strategy in wooing becomes essential. But I say the best wooing is natural."

ELEMENT 15 · · ·

Compassion

The small group had been traversing the narrow trail for some hours. The way led along the steep side of a vast mountain. Thousands of feet below a river surged through a rocky course. As the pass was extremely narrow they had been traveling in single file. Then quite suddenly around a bend they came upon a bridge. It was a fragile rope affair that crossed the gorge and connected with the trail on the far side. Even in the moderate wind it was swaying noticeably.

The child started crying. "I'm scared," he sobbed. "I don't want to cross." There was no choice, however. The man studied the bridge briefly, then started out upon it. The webbing sagged and tilted under his weight, and he grasped the handrope tightly. "I can't do it, I can't," choked the child on the path. He picked the child up in his arms, and holding him tightly to his chest again started across the wispy rocking bridge. "It's all right," he repeated several times, calming the child as they moved out over the far distant river. The ropes creaked and twisted underfoot and the whole bridge angled away from the horizontal position into an alarming cant. The man kept going. "It's all right," he said to the child again, who was shaking. "I'm taking care of you. . . ."

Wooing, too, has its terrors. They are bred of the great need to be wooed, to be loved, to be held. In any wooing that continues over a period of time, a bond of trust is formed. Attached to trust is dependence: "I trust you, I depend on you." Wooing, therefore, carries an obligation. This trust must not be disregarded nor placed too heavily so that it becomes a burden; nor even, perhaps, too early. In the most painful time, when the wooing comes to an end between two people, the trust needs to be honored, compassion shown. One of us wants to end the relationship, but the other does not, and the dependence of the other on us is strong. Like the child on the bridge, the scared crying one must be helped, not abandoned; wooing demands it. Pain will be inevitable, but it will be a little easier to endure if the ending is kindly made, the wooer a guardian within the trust.

Endings happen only once, however, and there are many times in the cycle of wooing when one of two people will need a small lift. These moments should be obvious to the other, but strangely they are often missed. Men and women, both, describe incidents in which their dependence on another cried out for help, but none was offered.

The solution to this history of pain in wooing is *to become the guardian of wooing itself.*

To be the guardian of wooing is similar to any unwritten contract between people: You don't call the shot out if it was in, cheat in cards, read other people's mail, shortchange the customer. In wooing, you simply do not hurt, and if there is the inevitable pain of parting, then there is an obligation to see insofar as possible that it be salved.

If wooing is the hope of millions and there is suddenly to be a rebirth of it, then millions of people will open themselves up to chances of betrayal. Large betrayals of duplicity, little betrayals of thoughtlessness. An element of wooing, then, is to protect its precept, to assume all the responsibilities; to guard against an unnecessary tear, a lonely, frightened hour; and if the fright and tears must be there because an ending is at hand, to see that they are anticipated and muted by the warmth of understanding.

ELEMENT 16 · ·

The Center of Wooing

Most of us are ordinary people in a landscape of predictable work, similar days; stimulated on the surface by surface entertainments. If we have times of elegance and grandeur, they often take place in fantasy, in which we stride forth to battle giants, save loved ones from burning buildings. We even borrow from Walter Mitty *his* fantasies. Real life has few glories.

We scrape for a living, worry about mortgage payments and rent, shop for bargains in food. We make festive occasions of birthdays and holidays, overspend on presents, glow in the surprise of an unexpected gift. Then the gala meal is over, the guests depart, and we return to the familiar landscape of our days and the relief of our fantasies.

But there are occasions when we leave our ordinary world and become noble. Ironically, battle may be one. Ordinary people are stripped of their ordinariness. The breadth of life becomes visible, and while everyone is mortal in these moments no one is mundane.

Wooing is such an occasion.

Any parent knows the symptoms of adolescent love, when all a child's existence spins around a center of infatuation. All priorities and perspectives are recast. In the adult context a similar change takes place: an ordinary person is reborn into a new world. Man or woman, for each it is the same.

Longing for a moment of intensity, vulnerability and mystery, a great tremor moves him. He is alive because of *her,* and his dormant beauty is revealed. She does this to him, but little does she know her effect. She sees him on a Sunday or a Monday and sees the beauty in the man, but because she has created it she does not realize that without her—and before her—the beauty was hidden by ordinariness.

But *he* knows she has brought him to this curious and fair state, has made him intense; and he thanks her. He is living at the edge of himself; and he woos her. He is so intense that in his life he can be like God himself—the grandeur of all possibilities seems open to him, and he loves her for that. From a long, shallow valley with its village cluster of low, tiled roofs, he is the spire rising into the morning twilight.

This woman makes me great.

This man makes me great.

It is the center of wooing.

ELEMENT 17 · · ·
Tangled Richness

Niver show a woman that ye care the snap av a finger for her, an' begad she'll come bleatin' to your boot-heels!
        Rudyard Kipling,
        "The Courting of Dinah Shadd"

Wooing contains its own paradox. We want it to end. Courtship is filled with uncertainties: will it work out? does he *really* like me or is this just a game? why doesn't she say she loves me outright? It is filled with ambiguities: who is it that she is going skiing with? "I've been trying to call you all evening, but the line was always busy. Who were you talking with?" It contains the pains of longing. And these do not have to be the agonies of full-blown unrequited love. The desire to express a thought and to be unable to because the wished-for recipient is unavailable causes an internal tempest. Hearing a song, "our song," on the radio, combined with the great urge to look into eyes not present, can create a crunching pain. We curse ourselves when we've forgotten, or were too fearful, to say something we had meant to, and we would give anything for the opportunity to relive the moment and speak the words. Barbs to the memory of chances lost or botched wear upon us.

In love, the longings can be crippling. William Meader, in his study of courtship in Shakespeare, describes the symptoms of *hereos,* the illness that traditionally comes to all who fall in love. Thus Valentine speaks of the ailment in *Two Gentlemen of Verona*:

> *Whose high imperious thoughts have punish'd me*
> *With bitter fasts, with penitential groans,*
> *With nightly tears, and daily heart-sore sighs. . .*
> . . . .
> *Love hath chased sleep from my enthralled eyes,*
> *And made them watchers of mine own heart's sorrow.*

Hereos can leave us tossing and turning, unable to sleep for anguish, yet it can also dull our minds to all else, so that we appear to be walking in our sleep. It can cause us to lose our appetite for food: Hamlet, rejected by Ophelia, "fell into a sadness, then into a fast, Thence to a watch, thence into a weakness, Thence to a lightness; and by this declension Into the madness wherein now he raves . . ."

If these dire circumstances surround unsettled love, the situation when one is partially smitten can be the same, in moderation; and in the earlier stages of wooing, less pronounced but no less real.

Yet, for all of that, we want the wooing to go on and on. "May it never end," said one woman who spoke of the by now clichéd agony and ecstasy of love. Being wooed is to be bathed in a warm, enveloping sense of being the center of someone else's thought. No one wants that special euphoric experience to come to an end. It is perhaps one reason why many affairs that began romantically and grew in ardor soon fell apart: the longing was over.

In Maine there is a joking comment made to the man who has just purchased a new boat (only it is not a joke): "There are just two days you will enjoy that vessel—the day you bought it and the day you sell it." In wooing there is the dizzying moment of the encounter when recognition of the other's interest is felt by each of two people. Later there is the death of what during an interim time perhaps became a painful experience. Most people can conjure this memory of a wooing. The ending is enjoyed for the closing it brings to anguish, yet it is also regretted because the pain carried its brother, pleasure.

Sweet agony. *"Odi et amo."* "O heavy lightness, serious vanity. Feather of lead, bright smoke, solid fire, sick health." Thus the paradox of wooing is defined. We hold on to wooing for the sweetness and accept the agony. It is a tangled richness that should not be disregarded completely or too quickly.

What, then, is the end of wooing? Once you are crushed in an embrace? When mouths first lock in a searching kiss? In sexual union? Marriage?

Wooing ends in a painful way when someone says or demonstrates "I do not want you." During the preparation of this book numerous people have also stated that marriage brought an end to wooing.

Some women even feel that wooing ends when they say yes or declare that they feel the same love that is being shown to them.

August. A moonlit night. Cruising aboard a sailboat. The wind dies, the engine is turned on but does not catch. The man climbs down into the engine well and starts to undo the fuel line, asking the woman for wrenches and other tools, which she passes down as he needs them. He has been wooing her for months. After an hour he gets the engine going, and then, still covered with blackened grease and oil, he says, "Will you marry me?"

She does not reply immediately. Long after the fact (she accepted), she says the pause was caused by the feeling that once she had said yes, the wooing would be over. "I was very aware of enjoying the proceedings, the wooing. On the other hand, if it had gone on *too* long something else would have intruded. After another *year* of the courting relationship I might have thought that he didn't really love me. There is a natural rhythm to these things, I think. But at that moment I wanted to extend time."

Uncertainty is a difficult subject to write about, analyze, comprehend, not to mention experience. Uncertainty is not normally a state we choose. By definition it is a tunnel of doubt, questions, nervousness, discomfort.

It is contradictory to all the other elements of wooing. Attention, recognition, the grand gesture—all are declarations without ambiguity. They are natural expressions that, for the recipient, promote the alleviation of doubt, question, nervousness, insecurity, discomfort.

In most activities we eschew uncertainty. The businessman attempts to prevent it, weather forecasters are hired to eliminate it (and fail). Gamblers live with uncertainty but wish they could overcome it through clairvoyance or mathematics.

Personally, I loathe uncertainty. It makes negotiations agonizing. I structure the activities of my days just to avoid ending them with uncertainty. Arguments that are not resolved are thorns in the mind that prevent sleep and puncture creativity. Uncertainty is the monkey on my back. It is ironic, therefore, that it should be my wife who puts forth the argument that uncertainty is an *essential* element of wooing, that for all the espousals of affection—signals sent to communicate, "I like you, I am wooing you"—uncertainty must remain part of the mix for wooing to proceed.

Perhaps it is true. In the Garden of Eden there existed a perfect state of equilibrium. Harmony and peacefulness prevailed. All needs had been anticipated and were gratified. There was no possibility of disharmony or disequilibrium. Adam and Eve could have no awareness of desire, just as they had never experienced separation or been aware of sexual differences. In this paradise there was no denial, no uncertainty. Adam and Eve had everything—except wooing—a concept, an activity conceived in post-Garden days, when Man must work for what he wants.

People do enjoy a degree of mystery, of challenge, of the hunt, of the game in wooing, which is perhaps another way of saying that they do want some uncertainty. "I don't think that one's primary drive is simply to be satisfied," says my wife. "It used to be the theory that what people wanted was to have all needs and desires immediately satisfied. A state of equilibrium was thought to be the goal: to avoid the extremes of cold and heat, pain and danger. The recent theory holds the opposite: that people don't want this middle road, or anyway, not for long."

Theories come and go, but there is some evidence to support this last one. People enjoy tension, which in wooing is equal tension for both. A woman does not want to be a fish with some man acting as the fisherman in control; nor does she want to be the fisherman in control of some man on the end of the line. Wooing must be mutual, with both being able to cause uncertainty and to be uncertain. People who read romance books certainly do not want the blandness of equilibrium; they thrive on the intensity of uncertainty. It is what makes them keep turning the pages. In most of these books we know the ending before we read the first paragraph. The books are purchased for the thrills encountered in following the hero and heroine through their tortuous path to union.

Many people say that they have better sex with their mate after a real fight. Is this because the fight is a dramatic departure from equilibrium? If the Pill heralded a temporary end to wooing, perhaps the cause is contained in the same point. The Pill provided a sense of equilibrium: sex with anyone, anytime. The threat of unwanted pregnancy was removed, and with it the need to abstain. Why deny oneself the pleasures of sex, any more than one denies oneself a good meal or a hot bath? The challenges were swept away.

Uncertainty in wooing, like uncertainty in anything, must be genuine. If the uncertainty is created artificially, as in some calculated wooing, it will not serve the purpose. Uncertainty is a time of torture, but is romantic too. Even though it is torture, it is pleasant. Mary does not mind that George does not call. She *wants* him to call, but she uses the time during which he does not call to think about him and about herself, to wonder if he is thinking about her and when he will call. And she thinks he ultimately *will* call. The timing of the call must be honest, and then it is wooing. It is fun because of the many, many swings between doubt, hope and a simple phone call. A woman called me to announce that she was going to be married. "Wonderful," I said, and continued: "I am writing a book about wooing. Tell me about that." "Oh," she replied, "the wooing is over." I asked another woman, married with four children, to give me her thoughts about wooing. Wistfully, she said, "I can't; it's been too long." Too long.

Does wooing really have to end then—with commitment? No, I believe it does not. But the fact—

which is a sad fact—is that the wooer may continue what earlier was wooing but now has become a part of a performance expected by the "wooee"; and the reciprocity ends. The flowers, the gestures, no longer bring the glad response they once did. Or the flowers and the gestures themselves may stop.

Says one who has been married for some time: "Wooing lasts only until you get what you want (or fail altogether). But what is it you want? Of course wooing continues after the sack, or you might not get in the sack again. You have to keep it so it goes beyond sex, keep on with the wooing right on through marriage up into old age, so it doesn't just become convenience, or less, just sexual convenience.

"However, once married, wooing does not continue in the same vein. After that what is important to keep alive is romance. I am very aware of specific romantic times with my husband. Sometimes they are similar to times we had before. A mirror. But that doesn't alter the fact that it is romantic. I think one form of wooing has to die, because you are giving everything anyway and if you wanted something, even a sign of affection, you can go straight at it and ask. But if the romance dies, which is wooing's partner, then the marriage doesn't work.

"I can't imagine what my husband would woo me for. Wooing has a purpose, to get something: acknowledgment, sex, an innate desire for a number of things—reciprocating feelings and the like. But I am very aware of romance."

My wife and I recently celebrated our twenty-fifth wedding anniversary, and I asked her if uncertainty was still part of the mix in our life together. "I hope not!" she replied. But according to her definition, then, we can no longer be wooers. I believe this is actually only a problem in semantics, of definition. If all the other elements—attention, gestures—are present in a marriage, I believe that the fundamental wooing is still in place. With this provision: The elimination of uncertainty cannot be turned into "taking for granted." To be taken for granted is a pernicious thing. Between two people, this attitude will bring on a withering of vitality. If a mate becomes a possession, then why bother? And in due course the impulse and the respect will become dulled, and with their disappearance will go romance and perhaps even love.

Boredom is the orphaned child of wooing that has died. Certain aspects of wooing will naturally be altered in a long-term liaison. The ambiguities and uncertainties leave. That is part of the solidarity of a marriage. However, if the fundamental bestowal of respect should lapse, there will be an invitation to slovenliness. Not only can we forgo the bother of the effort to look well and be alert to the other person's hopes, but we can become logy in the very emotions about which the bonds were tied.

Little is written about the aftermath of wooing—a few stories, operas—but from real life there are few clues. They are expunged from the memory. About the courtship that ended badly or sadly we tend to be revisionist: It never really happened, she was only flirting, he never really cared.

Isn't it strange and sad that so much emotion should be scrubbed away? The electric moments, like voltage, come with the speed of light and then are gone. Yet during the wooing every detail is registered. The tone of voice of the bid good-night, the fact that the fudge was hand-made, at what time of day the phone call came, the selection of a postcard. But when it has all washed by and the wooing is over—either because the partnership dissolved or was alloyed—the good-bye, let alone the tone of voice, is forgotten, the fudge unrecalled, and the postcard. . . . Ah, the postcard. Tucked away, it too is forgotten until years later when it is unearthed during spring cleaning. Then there is a quick melancholy flashback, and the card goes into the trash.

However, such an ending is not inevitable. As the final chapter of this book argues, wooing in its broadest sense need never end.

FIVE · · · ·

THE HAPPY ENDING

· · • • · ·

Has he no time for such things, as you call it, before he is married,
Would he be likely to find it, or make it, after the
  wedding?
That is the way with you men; you don't understand us, you cannot.
When you have made up your minds, after thinking of this one and that one,
Choosing, selecting, rejecting, comparing one with
  another,
Then you make known your desire, with abrupt
  and sudden avowal,
And are offended and hurt, and indignant perhaps,
  that a woman
Does not respond at once to a love that she never
  suspected,
Does not attain at a bound the height to which you
  have been climbing.

This is not right nor just: for surely a woman's affection
Is not a thing to be asked for, and had for only the
asking.
When one is truly in love, one not only says it, but
shows it.
Had he but waited awhile, had he only showed that
he loved me,
Even this Captain of yours—who knows?—at last
might have won me, . . .

Henry Wadsworth Longfellow,
The Courtship of Miles Standish

In the cycle of all living things the primal drive is
to live, survive. At one of its most fundamental levels
this will is the engine of reproduction. The environment places constraints on this drive. The environment is not a paradise—competitive forces are in
constant motion, disrupting and challenging the primal need. Thus natural selection alters and refines the
existence of all living things. But most living things
have their strategy to survive. A particular flower
presents a scent and an appearance designed to attract
the specific insect that will ensure its pollination.

Wooing is our way of releasing the innate drive to
achieve the relaxation of intimacy. "I know what she
gives me and I woo her for that. I also know what
she wants and I try to give it to her. That is my wooing." It is a survival strategy in a world of insecurity.

Woo well and life intensifies. By "woo well" is not
meant the execution of any measured technique. To
woo well means only to woo truly, without artifice

or a sense of self-primacy. If we woo well we survive, not as a threatened species exactly (and yet perhaps), but in our own unique human need of psychic fulfillment.

Woo well and life intensifies.

A day without luster is transformed by the simple reminder from someone you care for that you are the center of that person's thoughts.

Woo well and life intensifies.

With all the emphasis on sex, women have lost. The priorities have gone askew. A women gives away intimacy, is happy to do it, eager even. She protects her sexuality and gives that away last, believing that it is the plum, the golden ring, the ultimate reward. But in intimacy lie the treasures, the secret fantasies, private thoughts, favorite things. Sex is only an element of intimacy and a woman who gives her intimacy to a man has truly given him everything. Men often fail to understand this and women misunderstand it, believing that the gift of sex is paramount. In this way women have lost. Women have been deprived, and so men, too, have lost, because living in more shallow days has denied them riches.

Wooing will redress that imbalance.

Anna: "When you ask, Is not the word 'wooing' old-fashioned? All I can say is I don't know what it is, except that I want to be wooed. All women want to be wooed. Women are not loved enough. A man doesn't have to *buy* me something. It is such *little* things that are important. I want reassurances, that's all. I think that is what we all want. The man who knows that and acts on that is going to be wooing women at every turn whether he means to or not.

"*It is so simple, it's not even funny.* I am not insecure and I don't think most women are desperate with insecurities, although some are, and maybe I have been at times. So it's not that I am looking for reassurances of the kind a therapist might give. But when a man, through a simple action or statement, does give me reassurance I am moved because he is a man and I am me."

Woo well and there is a chance for splendor.

A thing worth doing is worth doing even badly. "Well" embraces "badly" when the intent is right. Do it.